LIFE WOULD Suck WITHOUT YOU

a girlfriend
MEMOIR

JENNIFER PREUSS

Copyright © 2017 by Jennifer Preuss

All rights reserved. No part of this publication may be reproduced, distributed, or transmitted in any form or by any means, including photocopying, recording, or other electronic or mechanical methods, without the prior written permission of the publisher, except in the case of brief quotations embodied in critical reviews and certain other noncommercial uses permitted by copyright law. Published by Facetious Publishing, Los Angeles, California.

Preuss, Jennifer
Life Would Suck Without You : a Girlfriend Memoir / Jennifer Preuss.

ISBN-10: 0-9989193-0-6
ISBN-13: 978-0-9989193-0-0

First Edition
Created in the United States of America

Facetious

Dedicated to my Cecil, my Lamb, and my Nooch
(my heart, my soul, my blood)

Life

"I heard you could use a friend." I was rehearsing the line over and over again in my head.

I was speeding down Reseda Boulevard to see my estranged best friend, Cecilia. The last time we spoke was 2008. We still shared a housekeeper, though, and that's how this all started.

Maria came over to my house that morning. This was weird because her usual day was Thursday. She just showed up. My kids were playing in their playroom when the doorbell rang.

"Jenny, I need to talk to you." She looked upset.

"Sure Maria. Come on in."

I opened the door, and we went into the kitchen. I had no idea what she was going to say to me. Was she being deported? Was her son in trouble? The next words out of her mouth were not what I would have guessed in a million years.

"Jenny, I have to tell you something. God is telling me in my heart that I have to tell you this."

"Maria, you're freaking me out. What is it?"

"Jenny, Chris has cancer. He is in the hospital. It doesn't look like he is going to make it."

What? No! This wasn't happening. Chris has cancer? He's thirty-three! I hadn't seen Chris and Cecilia in two years! This couldn't be possible. I knew what I had to do.

"What are you doing right now? Can you watch the kids?" I asked.

"Go. Now. I am here," Maria said.

I was driving over to Chris and Cecilia's house for the first time in two years. Would Cecilia slam the door in my face? Would she yell? Maybe she'd pretend she didn't even know me. Their daughter for sure would not remember me, even though I was there the day she was born. I changed her diapers, helped Chris and Cecilia get her on a sleep schedule, babysat when they needed extra help when they both had to be at work.

I can't believe I am about to see Cecilia. It's not like she didn't try to reach out. She called on my kids' birthdays and mine. Every time I saw her name come up on caller ID, I hit ignore. I had nothing to say to her.

But this ...

This was different.

Cancer? No. It's not possible. He's so young. How could he have cancer?

I pulled up to her townhouse complex. It was then that I realized I had to call her from the call box to have her let me in. This ought to be awkward. What was I going to say?

"Hi Cec, it's Jen, your old best friend who you haven't seen or spoken to in two years."

I got out of my car with as much courage as I could muster. I walked to the call box. I pressed her code and it started ringing. My heart was racing.

"Hello?"

"Cec, it's Jen."

"Oh, hi! Let me buzz you in."

That was easy. Maybe this wasn't going to be bad after all. I walked into the complex. I was trying to stay calm and take steady breaths. My heart was racing even faster now, and I thought I might hyperventilate. My fingers were even nervous. You know, the tingly, shaky feeling you get when you are about to do something you never thought you would ever have to do?

As I walked to her unit, I took a final deep breath. I stared at the unit number on the wall. 59. I lifted my shaking hand and knocked. It was now or never. The door opened.

"I heard you could use a friend," I said.

"Oh my God," Cecilia said, "Jen."

She reached for me, and we embraced. We stood in the doorway for what felt like hours but must have been just a few minutes. We swayed back and forth as both of us cried on each other's shoulders. Camille, who was three at the time, stared her big, beautiful, blue eyes at me. She must have thought I was a complete stranger. I guess I was to her at this point.

What had I done? How could I let these people slip away from me without a fight? I was living with the regret of my choices. I never claimed to be a good person and certainly this silence we had for two years wasn't *my* best self.

We sat down, and I had to ask.

"Did you know I was coming over? Did Maria tell you I was coming?"

"No! I thought you were my neighbor, Jen, who always gets locked out of the complex, so I buzzed you in. We were about to leave and heard the knock at the door."

Well, that explained how easy it was to get into the complex.

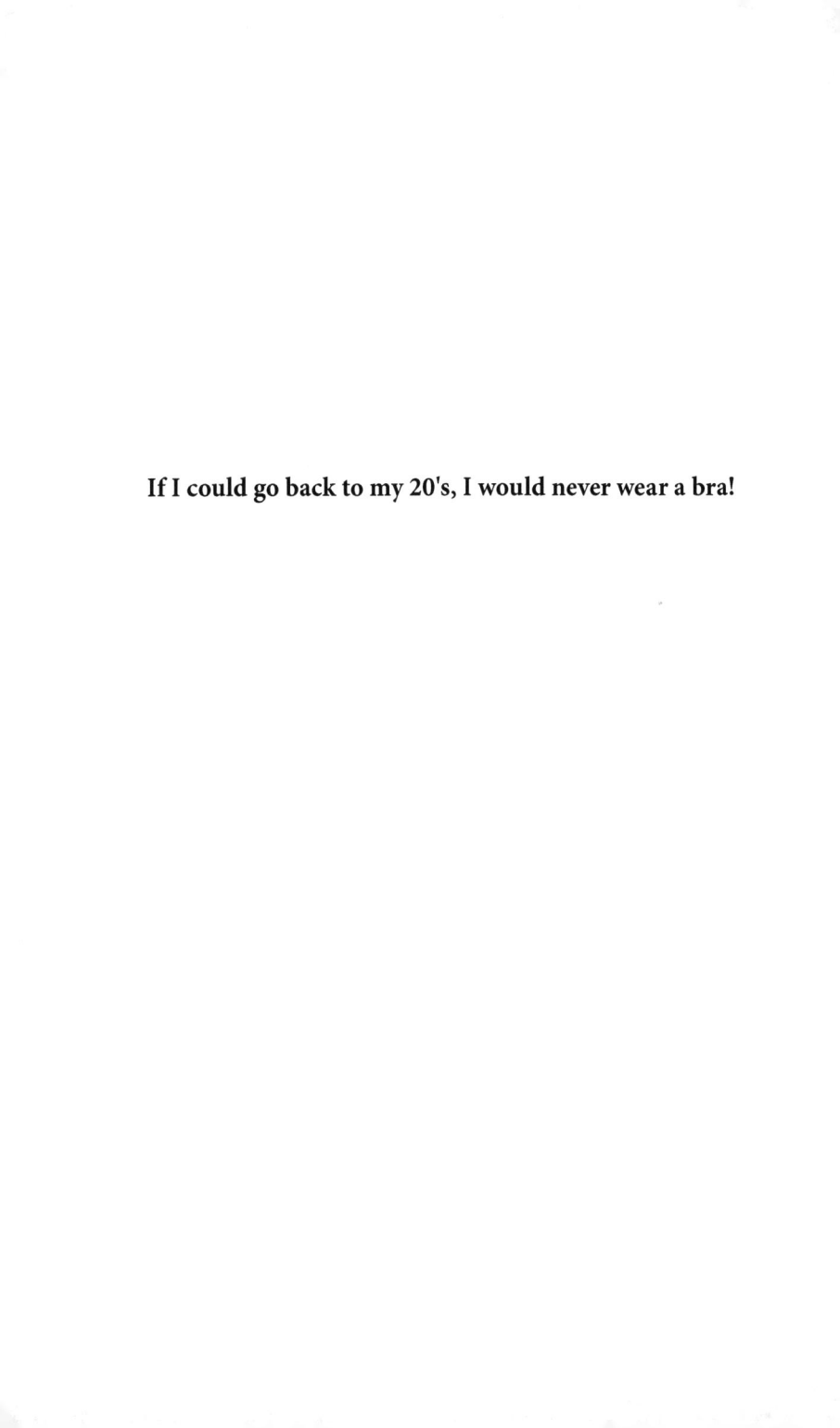

If I could go back to my 20's, I would never wear a bra!

Chapter One

Perhaps I should back up a little bit. I moved to Los Angeles from Philadelphia, by way of Miami for college, to be a soap opera star. Yes, that's right. Most people who want to act dream of being a movie star or landing on a sitcom. Not me. I wanted to be on General Hospital. The year was 1999. My first job was waiting tables at Houston's Restaurant in the Century City Mall.

"Full hands out!" That's what we shouted as we exited the kitchen at the Century City Houston's Restaurant. That meant we didn't have an empty hand to take anything out for anyone to his or her tables. There were so many rules you needed to know at this restaurant. It was unlike any other waiting tables job I had ever had. I worked at many restaurants as a hostess and server since I was sixteen. Very much a people person, I loved interacting with my customers. Only they weren't customers at Houston's. They were my guests. No. They were the restaurants' guests and me, nothing but a humble servant. It was my first week without shadowing a trainer, and it was overwhelming, to say the least. We only had a three-table section. This should be easy.

In college, I had six, sometimes seven tables in my section and I prided myself on my excellent service. But Houston's was unlike any other restaurant I had ever worked. It was run like the military. I will never forget ordering someone's lunch on the computer and hyperventilating because I had to get drinks to table 33, a "guest request" to someone not in my section (still my responsibility, though), and ring in a long order with more modifications than ingredients. As I tried to run out of the kitchen to get the guest request to the table, the manager shoved two plates in my hand reminding me not to leave the kitchen without full hands. When I arrived at *my* table, they yelled at me for not having their drinks. I promised to check on them.

"This might sound silly, but I can get back here much faster if you give me your empty bread plates to carry to the kitchen," I said. They looked at me like I was insane as I grabbed the untouched plates so I could have "full hands in" and made my way back to the kitchen. A manager stopped me and would not let me into the kitchen because I did not have FULL hands! Bread plates or "tip plates" as they were called, were small enough to grab other things. I scurried around the restaurant trying to find plates that needed clearing so I could get back to the drink area to make sure my drinks were going out to my table. I was so overwhelmed. I wasn't sure how much more of this I could take. Maybe I wasn't cut out to wait tables in Los Angeles? I found a few more big plates to clear and got back to the kitchen. When I put the plates down, I started crying. Like "ugly girl" crying.

A tap on my shoulder got my attention, and I turned around. This short, spunky looking girl with a pixie haircut was staring into my eyes. She pulled me close. Was this girl hugging me? She smelled good, like strawberries or something. How did she smell so good? I feel like I smell like I took a bath in BBQ sauce and salad dressing and I look like shit, and this girl is so put together. So adorable.

"Hey!" She said in a cute, clipped voice. "Everyone cries on the first day on their own! You've got this. Now put on a smile and go and get 'em, tiger!" She slapped me on the ass and shoved me out of the kitchen.

I couldn't stop from laughing. This perfect stranger just gave me a pep talk in the middle of a crazy shift and then slapped my ass in front of everyone.

After the shift was over, the chaos calmed down; I walked over to the little spitfire server. I wasn't sure what I was going to say. I wanted her to think I was as cool as I thought she was.

"Hi. What's your name?" I asked in my most casual voice.

"Nikki," she said.

"You're going to be my best friend!" I announced.

Some people wear 6-inch heels to walk around a farmers' market. Some people also wear those heels to take a flight lesson!

Chapter Two

WORK GOT INTO A routine. I learned the art of being a Houston's employee. Life was good. I had a boyfriend, some friends, and a job. I am a creature of habit and love routine. I think that's why I never ended up being successful as an actress. The lifestyle was too unpredictable. For now, I was holding steady with the life I was building for myself so far away from home. And that's when I met Panooch. We met while working at Houston's too. She was one of the three Nicoles, and I was one of the eight Jennifers. She called me "G," and I called her Panooch.

Panooch and I love to cook together. That's what I think drew us together in the first place. Nicole is a fashion forward kind of gal. On any given day she is dressed in high heels, full on make-up, blue eyeliner, long lashes, and pouty lips, she is always beautiful. She's my friend who loves me for who I am and sees the best in people. She is spiritual and loves talking about zodiac signs being the reason why certain people get along and why they don't.

"Oh, they're a fire sign and water sign. I give that relationship two weeks!" Panooch once tried to teach me how to walk in high heels. Needless to say, I wear lots of flats! It's not that she was a bad teacher. I think her student is seriously challenged.

"G! You have to actually lift your foot!"

"Like this?" I lifted my foot like I was doing a high knee in an exercise class. I looked ridiculous. I needed to wear high heels to a benefit that my husband was going to for work. At the rate I was going, I might as well go barefoot.

"Ok, listen Babe, you have to lift slightly. Point with your toe and slide forward. Watch." I focused on her feet and observed her as she modeled how to do this. How did she look so great doing it? I looked like a four-year-old trying to wear her mom's shoes. I tried again and slipped on the tile in my kitchen.

"Ugh! This is pointless! I'll never be able to do this by the weekend! We should have started these lessons five years ago."

"G, maybe this is because you're a Gemini. You know the twins are opposites. Today you're channeling the twin that can't walk in heels. I know! Let's try ballet slippers; they're really in right now."

Panooch and I also love to try new restaurants together and celebrate our birthdays even though it is never at a time when it is our birthdays. This is our thing. This tradition of ours is still observed each year, at random times, gifts and all, we go out for each other's "birthday."

Side Note: Everyone confuses her with Nikki because they have the same name. Both are beautiful, and both have dark hair. Honestly, I love them both to death but they are very different, and I do not understand why people get them confused. Nicole was a popular name in the '70s I guess but so was Jennifer (Hence the three Nicoles and eight Jennifers at Houston's)! Besides, the only person who calls Nikki "Nicole" is her mom when she is yelling at her to pick her dress off the floor and stop dragging it. So to help you, Nikki is always Nikki. She's the spunky server who slapped my ass and became my best friend in an instant. Nicole is Nooch or Panooch, who I also met waiting tables. Panooch is my super trendy, hippie-dippy, tarot card reading, animal lover with 6-inch Louboutin shoes best friend. Glad we got that cleared up.

On this one particular day we were in Pasadena, where parking sucks … just like everywhere in LA! This was not too long after I got engaged and was so excited to discuss wedding plans. I was trying to find parking, and it was impossible.

We were on the opposite side of the street when a spot opened. To snag the spot before anyone else, I made a U-turn, which I realized was illegal because a man in blue told me so. Thankfully it was a cop in a car.

Have you ever noticed how motorcycle cops are so angry? Do you think it's because they're bitter they don't get a car? Maybe they need air conditioning. Maybe they need a hug from their mother! I have never met a motorcycle cop who is nice.

I heard the sirens and saw the flashing lights.

"Fuuuuuuck!" I said in a whiny voice.

It was that moment of dread where your emotions all of a sudden get Bipolar Disorder. You start to think:

"Why did I do that?"

"Where's my time machine and can I have a redo?"

"I can't believe I just got caught when so many people are out there committing REAL crimes."

"I JUST WANT TO PARK MY CAR!!!!"

"I am so fucking stupid."

"I think I'm going to cry."

The officer walked over to my car and asked for my license and registration. If I let the cop walk away, I knew he was going to start writing me the ticket. Did you know once they start to write the ticket, they can't stop? Stupid rule.

Operation: *Keep Man in Blue at the Car* had officially started.

I had two things on my side. One, my best friend, my Nooch, is one hot piece of a$$. Two, when in the moment, I can pull off the performance of a lifetime. Talk about high stakes. If my college acting professors could see me now. They always talked about high stakes, and I felt those high stakes as I fought for my life to not get this ticket.

I explained to the young officer (No tears yet. You have to let that shit build.), "Officer, I am so overwhelmed. This is my one day off! I work two jobs just to make ends meet. My parents are going to kill me." I checked his face to see if he was buying it. He just stared at me. So I continued. This time I would try to be honest.

"Look, I am sorry. I made a mistake. I didn't see the 'no U-turn' sign until after I completed the U-turn." My voice started to shake. Nicole just sat there and watched me as I gave my Academy Award winning performance (Although, was it acting or desperation? I had a $300 ticket over my head. If I had to pay $300, the next two days at work would be community service, basically.)

I continued, "Can't a person make one mistake? Am I to be judged on a one-time, first offense thing? All I need is some compassion." Cue the sobbing. It was building, but now that dam had burst.

"Officer, you don't want us to think you don't have compassion. Do you, Officer? I mean you seem like an understanding guy. I'm sure you have a wife or sister that if in my position, you'd want them to have a second chance, right?" (Sniffle, sniffle … Nooch handed me a Kleenex and rubbed my back.)

He let me go with a warning! It worked! I am sure it was more that he wanted me to shut up and get away from me, but no ticket! It must have been my day!

Lunch was delicious!

I was always the designated driver in college.

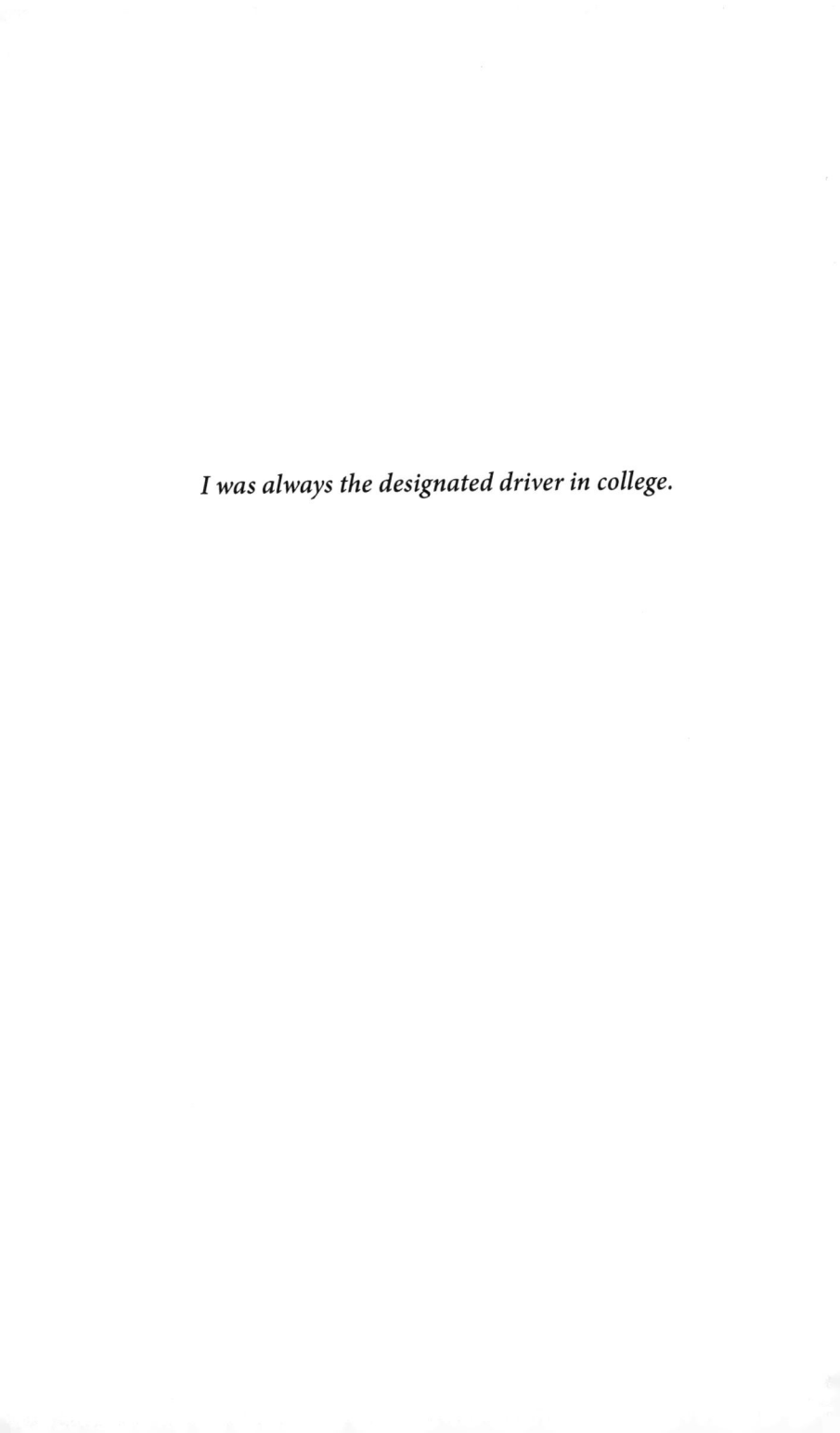

Chapter Three

"I DON'T THINK HE'LL EVER propose," I said sobbing into the Pottery Barn, tweed couch. Nikki was playing with my hair.

Nik and I spent the day hanging out, and it was almost time for me to go and get ready for a shift at Houston's. Nikki had just gotten married to her now ex-husband, but at the time I envied what they had. And it had me convinced that Rich was NEVER going to propose.

"Jeeennn." She said exaggerating the "e" sound in my name, drawing it out in her deep, authoritative voice and rolling her eyes. "He'll do it when he's ready. You don't want to rush this."

But I was in a rush. I didn't want to get married in my thirties. I wanted to be a young mom. I had a plan and had to stick to it.

Little did I know that afternoon, when I went to work, Rich called Nikki and asked her if she wanted to see the ring! We got engaged the next day. Panooch and her boyfriend at the time came over with a bottle of champagne to celebrate. Nikki was at a party and came over after to say, "I told you so."

now, all these months later, it was time to
y wedding was just a few months away. I was
g the man of my dreams. My Mother-in-law's
od best friend introduced us. She said he was
a director in Los Angeles and could help my acting career! We met for lunch while I was looking for an apartment before moving out here. He handed me a Thomas Guide, which was a book of maps for the city. Back then, this was our GPS, and everyone in LA had to have this in their car to get around. When he offered it to me, I started to laugh.

"You weren't going to give this to me if I was ugly, were you?" I said.

"Nope. I was going to have a new Thomas Guide," he replied laughing.

I knew we were meant to be. He got my sense of humor. We moved in together four months later and dated for two and a half years before getting engaged. And as far as my acting career was concerned, Rich was always supportive, but he works in live television. This was not a part of the industry that was searching for struggling actors. At least I got to marry him!

Nikki threw me a beautiful bridal shower with Rich's cousin. And that same night, she planned my bachelorette party. I remember Panooch bought Nikki a present to thank her for throwing me the party. It was like a mom thanking someone for being friends with her child.

Both Nikki and Nicole are good about knowing my limits. The two of them can party. Me ... not so much. I love to perform and be the center of attention.

I was a theater major after all. But I am just not good with staying up late. It doesn't take much to get me tipsy either. And ever since college I have never liked going to bars or clubs. I hate how people rub up against you or grab you on the dance floor. It's not that I'm a prude. I'm not. Most people who know me would be shocked to hear this. I am super outgoing and, like I said, I love attention. I just like being with people who I am comfortable with. Nikki and Nooch have always understood that about me and have never pushed me to do anything or go anywhere I am not comfortable. When it came to my bachelorette party, they got creative.

The night started at Nikki's apartment at 6:00 p.m. Nikki made up the cutest drinks named after characters from General Hospital. I did get on the show one time, as an extra, by the way. But that was the extent of my Soap Opera career. At least I had my Luke and Laura beverages.

Little did I know these drinks they made were all virgin drinks! I was high on life, apparently. I remember thinking, "Wow. I've built up a tolerance. I don't feel anything."

We played games. Nooch and I won the game for carving the most realistic penis out of a cucumber. I was rewarded with a pretty, satin bag to hang on my wrist. We all then loaded into the minivan that Nikki rented to drive around town. It was hysterical seeing her drive this huge van that was my "ride" for my epic evening out.

Our first stop was El Coyote, a Mexican restaurant in LA. It was there that I had to reach into my satin bag, on my wrist, and read a piece of paper out loud.

"Get a guy to buy you a shot." No problem. It's not the same as going to a club. In a restaurant with my best friends ... I could make a fool of myself. I walked right up to a guy at the bar.

"Hey! I'm getting married, and it says on this paper here that you should buy me a shot!"

"Ok," he said. "Hey how about a shot of tequila for my friend here who is getting married," he yelled to the bartender.

That was easy! I was able to advance to the next place. We drove over to another bar that had a dance floor. No one was there because remember; we started early. The girls knew I wouldn't last long. We went out on the dance floor, and all danced together. It was so much fun dancing with my girls. Time went by, and it was now nine o'clock, and I had to take another paper out of my satin bag. This one said, "Get an entire bar to sing the Brady Bunch Theme Song." Ha! I have this. By now the bar was filling up, and I had to push my way through to lift myself up onto the bar. When I did, I got everyone's attention.

"Here's the story of a lovely lady who was bringing up three very lovely girls ..."

Everyone started singing with me. The entire bar was singing.

"The Brady Bunch. The Brady Bunch. That's the way we became the Brady Bunch."

I am quite the oxymoron. I love attention but don't want strangers to party with me at a club or a bar. I know I'm weird. But I felt so safe in this environment because I knew Nikki and Nooch were there to protect me. I can't feel uncomfortable when I'm with my girls. It's one of the things I most treasure about our friendship.

After that bar, we walked outside, and I had to pull another paper out of my bag. This one said, "Get a guy to beg you not to get married." This one was going to be tricky. We went outside, and there was now a line to get into this place. I walked up to a cute guy in line. I was holding Nooch's hand. Nikki went to get the van. I showed him the paper and smiled. I pointed to the tiara on my head that Nikki bought me for the night that said "Bachelorette." He got down on a knee and professed his undying love for me.

"Please … please" he shouted. "What's your name?" he whispered. I told him it was Jen. "Please, Jen. Don't do it! Don't marry him! Marry me instead. I am the man for you. I love you!"

Honk, honk! Went the minivan. Nikki pulled up just in time for me to let the guy "off" easy. I gave him a smile and a wink and yelled thank you, as Nooch pulled me to the van.

Last stop was a place called Crazy Girls. Yes, it's a strip club. I didn't want to go to a strip club where men strip. I wanted to look at hot girls with bodies I wished I had and knew that everyone at this place would have no interest in me because they were watching these hot chicks dance. I was rewarded with a shot for accomplishing all my chores for the night (So two shots for the night and a ton of virgin "General Hospital" themed drinks, and I was three sheets to the wind.)

"So pick a girl." Nooch and Nikki wanted to buy me a lap dance.

"I don't know. That one?" I said. I pointed to a blonde girl that was kind of plain Jane.

"No, G! That girl is a skank. You can't just go and pick the first girl you see! Wait for someone that's hot. Otherwise, it's not worth it." Nicole scolded me in her incredulous voice.

"Yeah, take your time. Make it count," Nikki chimed in.

I found a girl that was about 5'5" with dark hair. She was sweet and innocent looking. I pointed to her, and the girls started to giggle.

"That's who I would have picked too," Nooch said.

"Let's see if we can watch!" Nikki said.

Nikki approached the girl and talked to her. The next thing I knew, I'm in some room with a bunch of other guys sitting and getting a lap dance by their "Miss Not So Innocent." It was so uncomfortable. I thought I would like it. I mean, I pictured it in my head, and it was so much hotter than reality. Instead, this girl and I talked about our families. She was telling me about her brother and how he doesn't approve of her being a stripper. He was in medical school and judged her. It felt like a therapy session, and I was the therapist.

When it was over, Nooch walked me out to the van where Nikki was waiting.

"I'm proud of you, G. How was it?"

"She was underwhelming. Next time, we'll pick a less chatty one. Shut up and dance, Bitch!" Now, why couldn't I be that cool in real life?

I was asleep in the car in minutes and was home by 11:45. It was the perfect ending to my perfect bachelorette party.

Adult board game nights can be cut-throat

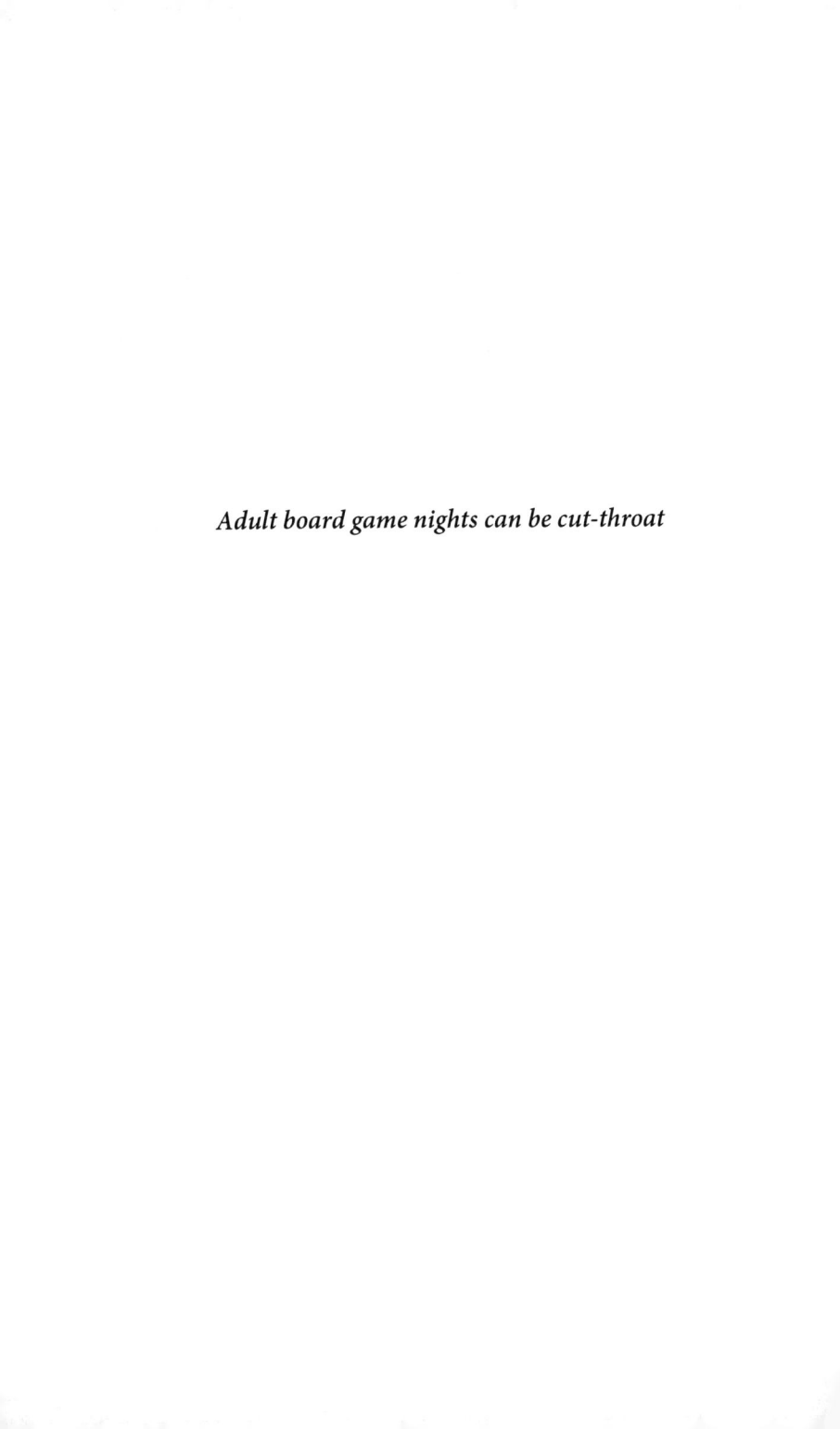

Chapter Four

AFTER WE WERE MARRIED, Rich and I moved to the Valley and bought our first home. It was a townhouse in Tarzana, California. It was hard to move away from where Nikki and Nooch lived, but life was moving forward and changing. We saw each other as much as we could. Nikki had landed a job traveling around the country as a television host. Nooch got a bartending job in Santa Monica. I was substitute teaching.

Chris and I met around this time at a school he and I were both subbing for. We were instant friends because we both had a love of Mexican food and Jack Bauer ("24" reference, if you don't know who that is and shame on you for not knowing). Cecilia, Chris's girlfriend, kept hearing about this "Jen" person and referred to me as his "work wife." One day Chris told me Cecilia was coming to visit the school to meet me. I was like, right. She's coming to check me out!

"Who is this girl spending all this time with my boyfriend?" She had to have been wondering.

Well, we met and hit it off. The next day was a Saturday, and we made plans to go to the mall together while my husband and Chris watched a game on

TV and had a beer.

We got to the mall at eleven in the morning and came home at eight at night. We were in love! The rest was history. We were soul mates from the start, and I thank God every day that I met Chris and he gave me Cecilia.

"If I had to lose my best friend, at least I lost her to my wife," Chris said at their wedding.

Cecilia and I were inseparable. We have been known to title our times together. For example, *The Summer of The Notebook* or *The Day of Bed, Bath, & Beyond*.

The Summer of the Notebook was when Cec was reading the epic love story *The Notebook* and got me obsessed with it. We would lie in the pool for hours and discuss, at great length, each scene of the book. I think we even read excerpts to each other while floating on pool rafts. It sounds silly now, but I am telling you, Noah and Allie were important people to us.

The Day of Bed, Bath & Beyond was a classic "Jen and Cec" day. We needed to go to Bed Bath &Beyond for something. I honestly can't remember what it was. I had a coupon and wanted an excuse to use it. We parked the car and were so engrossed in our conversation.

"Noah reminds me of this guy I was madly in love with in high school," I said.

"Which one? You've told me you were in love with so many; I've lost track."

"Well, what can I say? When I fall, I fall hard." I laughed at myself. "I think I just wish those guys loved me in return the way Noah loves Allie."

We sat in the car for an hour talking about different boys we liked when we were younger and detailed versions of our own epic love stories. We left the parking lot laughing at ourselves and decided to do a "drive by" to see if a boy Cecilia liked in high school still lived in the same house. Thankfully, no one saw us. All we did was drive by this guy's house and then took off. We thought we were so cool.

We then went home to hang out and watch a movie. When we got home and started the movie, it was then that we realized that we never even went in Bed Bath & Beyond to get what we were supposed to get!

It wasn't just Cec and me hanging, but all four of us. Rich, Chris, Cec, and I had dinners together, went to movies, celebrated holidays. Inseparable.

Cecilia fit in perfectly with Nik and Nooch too. We tried to make time for each other. We attempted to get together, just us four girls, to have dinner and catch up. We called it "Dinner with Life" since I always refer to these three girls as my "Life."

Most of the time, though, our weekends were double dates with Chris and Cec. Chris had studied in Japan for a year and so we would go out to those places that have Teppan grills or as I call them "Cook in Front of You Restaurants." I would always make Chris speak to the chef in Japanese and would get so excited when they would have a conversation.

It became a routine to go out to dinner and then hang out at one of our houses after. We lived on the same street, so it was convenient for hanging out. One night we went to dinner and came back to our house, and we decided to play a game called Scategories. Rich and I ran upstairs to change our clothes. We ate way too much and wanted to be comfortable.

As the game began, Chris would yell at Cecilia when she got an answer wrong. One of their turns got pretty heated when they had to, as a team, spell the word 'backwards' backwards, one letter at a time between the two of them. Chris started off.

"S," he said.

"D," Cec said.

"R," Chris said.

"Um. Um. W?" Cecilia questioned.

"God dammit Cec! It was 'A'!"

This was after they had been losing. Chris abruptly stood up and stormed out our front door without a word. Cecilia looked so confused and embarrassed.

"What do I do? Do I go after him? That was so bizarre," Cecilia said.

After seven minutes of debating what to do, there was a knock at my door. It was Chris. He was wearing sweats and a t-shirt. He threw a pair of sweats at Cec.

"Go change," he told her.

She did, and when she came out of my powder room, she sat down, and we all looked so confused.

"Now we're on an even playing field. They had the advantage because they were comfortable!" Chris said with a smirk on his lips. We all thought he was really mad. He left us sitting there dumbfounded for seven minutes. Anything to win. Jerk.

Life was easy. We spent hours laying by the pool

talking and then realizing it was seven at night and we had gone outside at ten in the morning. We never ran out of things to talk about, and if we didn't have anything to say, Cec and I sang songs that we both loved.

Sometimes we had handstand competitions in the pool. Rich and Chris would judge.

"I give that a six and a half," Chris said.

"What? That's bullshit! That deserved at least a nine! That shit was graceful!"

"Your legs were not as straight as they could have been."

Mimicking him in a baby voice, "Your legs were not as straight as they could be. Huh. I'll show him straight legs!"

Cecilia laughed at me.

I took a deep breath, jumped up and sank into the water, down to the pool floor. I placed my hands on the floor and pulled my legs into my stomach and hiked my legs up through the water. My legs were still like statues and as close together as they could get. My dismount was beyond graceful as I glided back down to the pool floor and emerged to the top of the water like Ariel the mermaid.

"That ... was a nine," Chris had a smirk on his face.

Cec chimed in, "Hey, let's do them at the same time. We could be the first synchronized handstand athletes at the Olympics!"

"Oh my God, we would win, for sure!" I said.

The rest of the day was spent perfecting our synchronized handstands. Chris was a tough coach, but he would get us the gold!

One time, our townhome's electricity went out. I had been upstairs reading. Rich was watching a movie downstairs. We decided to walk to Cec and Chris's to hang out.

Hours later, we came home. When we opened the door, we heard ominous moaning in the living room. I screamed thinking someone broke into our house. Turns out the power had come back on, and the movie Rich was watching was The Shining.

Chapter Five

ONE SUMMER AFTERNOON, I was home reading on my couch. Rich was at work. Cecilia was at work, too. I was getting into my book and relaxing when I heard a slithering sound. I froze.

"What the fuck was that?" I asked myself out loud. Yes, I talk to myself when I am alone.

I waited, frozen on the couch, hugging my knees to my chest. And then again, a slithering sound! My heart was pounding.

"Oh my God. There's a snake under my couch," I whispered this time. I carefully reached over to my end table for the phone and called Chris.

"A what?" Chris asked.

"A snake!"

"Jen, you're crazy. There is not a snake under your couch."

"I am telling you right now, Christopher, if you don't get over here this minute and catch this thing, I am going to be strangled to death and Rich will get home and find my dead, strangled body and be very upset that you didn't save me!"

Laughing he said, "He might thank me!"

"Chris!"

"OK, OK. I'm on my way."

"Come through the garage, you know the code, right."

"Yes. I'll be there in a minute."

I blew out the breath I was holding. Thank goodness. He may make fun of me, but I knew he loved me. Chris wouldn't want me to be eaten by a snake. I wonder how big it is? How did it even get into my house?

A couple of minutes later Chris came through the door that leads to my garage. He had a broom and a flashlight in his hand and took his shoes off. He signaled to me to be quiet. You know, the universal finger to the mouth. I nodded my head in agreement pointing under the couch I was sitting on. It was like we were in an episode of our favorite show, *24*. He was Jack Bauer rescuing me from a terrorist snake that invaded my townhouse.

Chris tiptoed towards me, and there was the noise again! It was louder this time. Chris jumped onto my coffee table, scared out of his mind. It was kind of hysterical. If I weren't so scared, I would have laughed out loud.

The noise came again, and Chris's expression changed. He got off the table and crouched down on the floor. Wow, he was brave now! He flashed the flashlight under and stuck the broom handle under there. Nothing.

"Jen, there's nothing under there."

"Oh no! It got away!" I was hysterical.

"No. There's nothing under there. I think your

neighbor is doing some work or something."

"What?" I picked up the phone and called next door to Larry and Marie's house. We shared a common wall. Their kitchen wall was my living room wall.

"Hi Larry, it's Jen from next door. Are you doing some work in the kitchen, maybe near the wall?"

"Oh, hi Jen. Yes, we're doing some plumbing.
Is it disturbing you?"

Oh, my God, I am an idiot. "No, no. Just curious what the, um, noise was. Sorry to bug you."

I hung up the phone and started to cry.

Chris gave me a hug. "If it makes you feel any better, I thought it was a snake too the first time I heard it."

When push came to shove, he was there for me. Chris and I walked back to his townhouse and hung out there. He went to get me Mexican food from our favorite restaurant. Cecilia came home and we told her the whole story.

"Wow! I am so glad Chris was able to rescue you!"

Some people have flat stomachs; I have a natural arch in my eyebrows

Chapter Six

Have you ever been embarrassed by your best friend? I mean, hide in between the clothing racks because she's screaming that Kate Spade is ripping everyone off and you can find better shit at Marshalls? Well, that's my Nikki. She's my feisty, honest, uninhibited girl. She says it how it is. Except it's embarrassing when she does it in the middle of Bloomingdale's—my place of worship.

After Rich and I started having kids, my free time was super limited, as you can imagine. When you start a family, no one tells you that you will not have time to do anything for yourself. Or maybe they do, but you don't listen. And if you're lucky enough to find a sliver of time, you'll spend it wondering what you should do with that time. When you decide on how to spend that time, the baby wakes up, or it's time to go pick up the other kid at preschool.

One day Nikki came over to my house to hang out, and I was in the shower. The baby was napping, and I had a few seconds to get myself together. She came into my bathroom to talk to me while I was showering. She looked at me.

"Oh no. Jen! What is going on with your cooch?"

She proceeded to tell me how having kids was no excuse not to vacuum the carpet.

"Nikki! I am a mom! I don't have time for shaving and grooming." I yelled.

"No, Jen. You are a person. You are not just someone's mom or wife or teacher. You need to take care of yourself and feel sexy and confident."

She's so hard to argue with. The next thing I knew, she went to CVS to buy me a special trimming razor. When she got back to my house she ordered me into the bathroom and was showing me how to groom myself! Most people think it's gross to hear this story, but honestly, it's just how our relationship is. I trust her. I am not embarrassed to be naked in front of her, and she did make a valid point. As I looked down at myself, I realized I *was* letting myself go. Sometimes it takes a friend to give you that smack in the ass that you need. Nikki has been doing that for me since day one, literally smacking my ass!

After the shaving incident, I was getting dressed when I offended her once more.

"What are those granny panties you are putting on?" Nikki yelled. "Geez. No wonder you never have sex. You're walking around like a hairy grandma," she added. "Where are your thongs?" She asked.

"Nik, I hate thongs. I don't like how they feel. I like full coverage," I said.

"You know everyone can see your underwear line with those things you are putting on," she said.

"There are far more offensive things in society

than you seeing my underwear line. My ass dimples, for example, might offend you greatly," I snickered.

Nikki laughed.

I continued, "I also believe that people who design underwear either don't wear underwear or are never in a rush!"

"Whaaaat?" Nikki said laughing.

"Do you know how many pairs of lacy underwear I have torn through getting dressed in a rush trying to stop the kids from fighting or because I was running late for work?" I asked.

"We are going to Victoria's Secret right now and getting you new underwear," Nikki said.

As we shopped, Nikki said, "I promise, you'll get used to it. You just need the right one. You won't even feel it."

She came into the dressing room with me.

"Ok, model for me," she asked.

I posed in various poses in my most awkward imitation of a Victoria Secret model. We were laughing and making model-type faces.

"Damn, now Richard will want to fuck the shit out of you! Clean cooch and hot underwear!" She announced to me and ALL of Victoria's Secret.

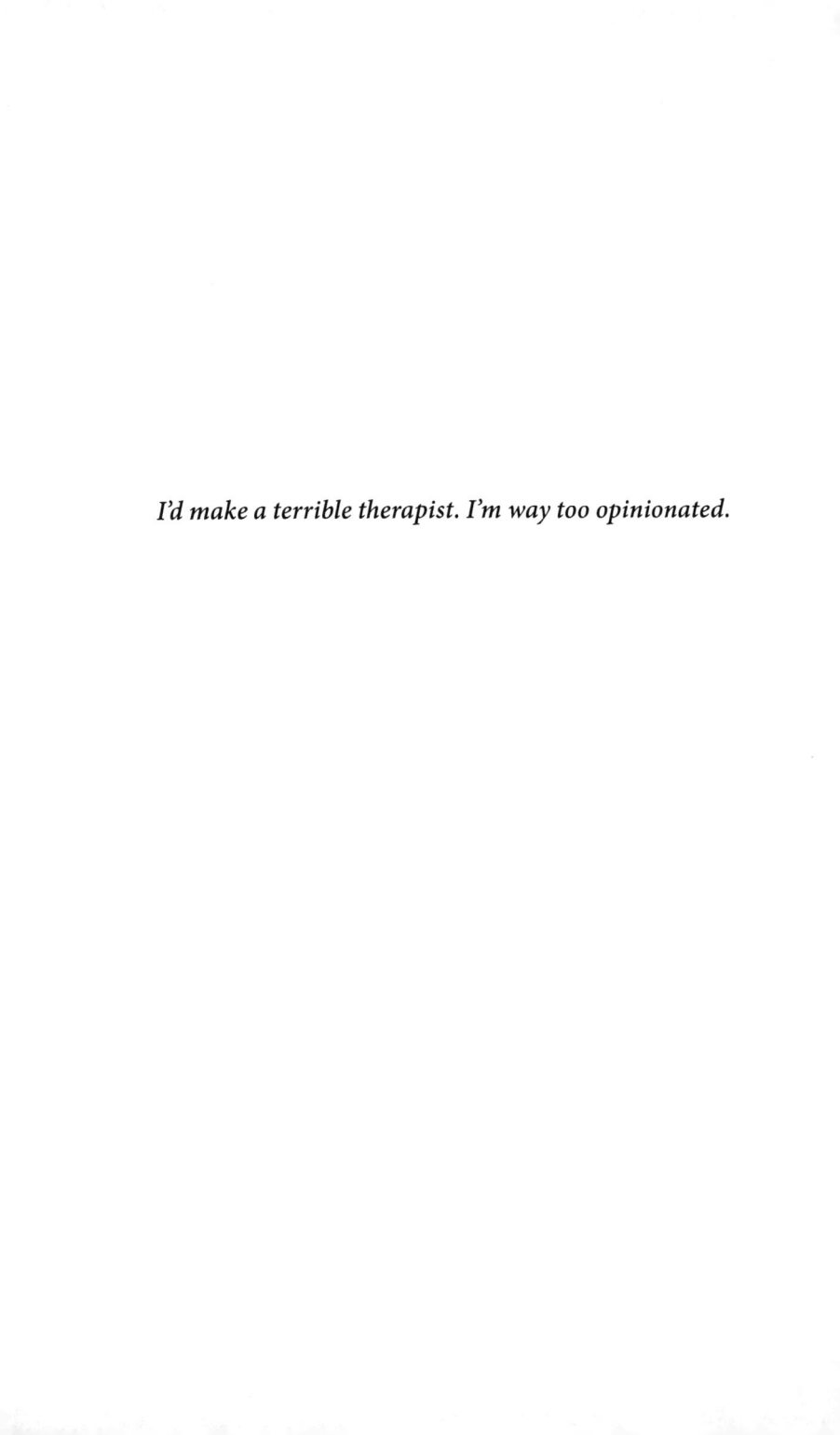

I'd make a terrible therapist. I'm way too opinionated.

Chapter Seven

Like I said before, Panooch and I became friends over our love of cooking. We loved to cook together, go to new restaurants, and watch cooking shows. We once waited for four hours just to meet Ina Garten, the Barefoot Contessa. Panooch is my "fancy" friend. She's always dressed to the nine's, so put together, and knows all the great places to go to eat and shop. She's a real class act. And she is wilder than I'll ever be. Secretly, I dream of being as free-spirited as she is but I know that my need to control everything would always get in the way.

I have always been on a timeline. I had to be married by a certain time, had to have kids by a certain time. Panooch is never in a rush. She knows what she wants out of life, a relationship, and herself. I think I have always been in such a rush to meet my own deadlines, that I am now trying to figure it all out as I go and I get resentful. One time, years before she met Marc, her husband, Panooch dated a guy who asked her if she would have a threesome with him and another girl. I was mortified.

"Obviously you told him 'No'!?!"

"What's the big deal? It could be fun." She was always up for something new and exciting. I guess I was a prude. I talk a good game, but when it comes to anything off the beaten path, I clam up. This is because of the Jewish guilt instilled in me at birth by my mother (Love you, Mom). I am always worried what she'll think of my choices. I guess that's not a bad thing. It kept me as the designated driver in college because I wouldn't drink underage. I was always the girl you could count on. I'll be there when the cows come home, or the saying goes.

Anyhow, I always admired the way Nicole lived her life. Until one day she told she went to this party with a mutual friend of ours. She was telling me there was cocaine. I went off on her. I couldn't have been more judgmental. I told her I was disgusted that she would partake in a party that had illegal drugs. And was she even considering trying it? It was an illegal drug! I have never done any illegal drugs (even smoking pot), and I was so naïve, I assumed that stuff didn't go on at parties. One time, at a Who concert, a seventy-year-old woman with long gray hair and no bra on was dropping acid next to me. I asked Rich if we should report it to the police. He never took me to another Who concert.

Another thing instilled in me from birth: Drugs are bad, and people who do them are gross. Needless to say, Nooch and I stopped talking. I think months went by. I had lots of time to reflect on my actions. This is where I learned my lesson. I mean, who the fuck was I to tell her what to do? She confided in me, and I didn't even give her a chance to tell me what her experience was like. Maybe she hated the party? Maybe she loved it? Maybe she didn't end up trying anything and if she did, who the hell was I to make judgments on it? The fact was, it wasn't my business what she did. All three girls had always accepted me for who I am. What kind of friend was I if I couldn't do the same? I couldn't let this go on. The silence was killing me. I decided to write her a letter.

I poured my heart into this letter. I told her how sorry I was for judging her and who did I think I was? I begged for forgiveness and told her my life was not as much fun without her in it. I never mailed it. By the time I was ready to mail it, she had called to make lunch plans. Apparently, she wasn't even upset with me. She didn't even know I thought we were in a fight. She just thought I had gotten busy and she was busy and why was I acting like we were in a fight? When I explained it all to her she brushed it off like only Nooch can.

"Oh that? I didn't do it G, and I know how you feel about that stuff. That's not why I didn't do it, but your reaction wasn't anything different than I expected you to have."

She wanted to have lunch that day because she met a guy named Marc (Yes, her now husband) and was smitten with this hot British man who stole her heart.

A long time passed after that. Marc and Nicole got engaged; our friendship went on like normal. One day we were supposed to have lunch when I got a phone call. It was Panooch. She sounded awful.

"G, I have the flu. I can't make it to lunch."

Of course I understood. I wanted to make sure she was OK because Marc was out of town shooting a movie.

"Do you need me to come over? I can bring you some soup?"

"No, my sister is in town this week. I'm fine. I just need to rest. Love you, Babe."

"Love you!"

The next day, she called again.

"G, I'm in the hospital. There's fluid around my heart, and the doctors don't know what's wrong. They don't think it's the flu. If you still want to have lunch, I have a private room at Cedar's."

She was trying to make a joke, but her voice was trembling. She had fluid around her heart, and the doctors couldn't figure out what was wrong?

Nikki was on her way over for dinner that night, but instead, I left her with my then 18-month-old son so I could go see Nicole at the hospital.

When I got there, she looked awful, pale, frail, and skinny. Marc was on his way from Vegas where he was shooting his movie. They were to be married in just two months.

"Thanks for coming, G."

"I wouldn't be anywhere else."

Just then the doctors came in. It was a team of doctors. They were called "The Blue Team." I'm not sure what "The Blue Team" did more than other doctors but they seemed important. Or maybe they were a group of residents following a doctor and blue was meant to be green, as in new.

They examined Nicole for a few minutes. While they were going over notes in the hallway, I stepped out to ask them a question.

"Doctor, if I wanted to help, what could I do?"

"Your friend needs a blood transfusion. You could donate blood."

"Done," I said.

"Nooch, I'm going downstairs to donate blood for you. I'll be back in a bit." Just then, Marc came barging through the door. He had just landed from Las Vegas and rushed over to the hospital. It was a sweet thing, seeing them together. Nooch cried and Marc held her tenderly. I knew she had found her soul mate.

"I'm going to give you two a moment alone and head down to the Blood Bank," I closed the door and headed downstairs to where you donate blood.

My Panooch was getting worse, and no one could figure out why or how to stop it. I had to do something.

I sat in the blood bank for three hours. First, I had to wait for an hour before my name was called. Then, I had to fill out a million papers. Then, they took my blood. Next, you have to wait until you've had juice, so you don't feel woozy. By then it was seven pm. I decided to go home. I did all I could do for the day, and Marc was with her now.

The next day, Nicole was transferred to ICU. At this point her mom flew in from Kentucky, Marc was there, and her sisters. She called me that afternoon, after going to ICU. She sounded so weak and tired.

"G, I just had a transfusion, and I think it was your blood. The bag was marked that it was donated specifically for me."

"I'm so glad, Nooch. How are you feeling?"

"I just woke up from a nap. I think your blood is very calming because I had a really good, peaceful nap."

I laughed. "Calm? My blood? Maybe it was from someone else. We all know I am anything but calm. I would think it would make you a spaz."

She started to laugh with me. It was good to hear her laugh, even though she still sounded weak.

"G," her tone was serious now. "This makes us blood sisters for life."

A tear rolled down my cheek. I dashed it away with the back of my hand, and I laughed, "Forever, Nooch. We're blood sisters for life. I love you." I told her I would call her later and let her get back to her rest.

The next day when I called to check on her and asked if I could do anything for her, she asked me to bring her sushi. Sushi? It couldn't be good for an ICU patient to have raw fish.

"I don't want my last meal to be chicken broth."

That's all it took for her to say. I rushed over to a sushi place across from the hospital, Sushi Roku. I bought one of everything (Of course, I made sure there was no mayo since I detest it and Nooch would expect nothing less from me.) When I got to ICU, I smuggled it in like it was an illegal drug crossing the border. I was rounding the corner to her room and ran right smack into her doctor. We exchanged looks. Quietly, I told him there was no way I was going to let a dying woman not have her last meal request. He shook his head and stepped out of my way, making a big gesture to cover his eyes. My secret was safe with him. It was that moment when I realized how real this all was. When the doctor was allowing me to bring in raw fish to an ICU patient, something major was about to go down.

I took a deep breath and walked into her room.

"G!" We hugged, and I set everything out in front of her. "Geez, G, did you get enough?"

"I didn't know which you wanted so I got a bunch."

"This isn't a bunch; this is the whole restaurant." We laughed, and I made a plate for her.

We ate our sushi together and Panooch looked happy for the first time in two weeks. Hospital food must suck, especially for a foodie like Nicole. The nurse came in and gave us the "Nurse Ratchet" look and then gave Panooch some medication. Marc and Nicole's mom were there and started writing something down.

"What are you writing?" I asked.

"We started writing everything they are doing and noting any changes for the better or worse."

"That's a good idea!" I said. Nicole had Ulcerated Colitis and they were giving her meds for that while she was in the hospital for this mystery illness that was slowly killing her.

Turns out, it was a brilliant idea! Every time they gave Nicole the colitis meds, her illness worsened. By a certain time of day when the medication wore off, Nicole would improve.

But every day when she took the medication, she got bad again. Marc insisted that they stop giving her the colitis meds and test it. As it turns out, her body had developed an allergy to the medication, and that was what was causing fluid around her heart! Crazy, right?

Within three days, she was released from ICU. A week later she was released from the hospital! She was saved! She could get married, have a full life, and I could still have my best friend! My life doesn't make sense without all three of my girls.

I was so done with hospitals. Or so I thought.

"Oh, and you're welcome"

Chapter Eight

One time I was so sick and couldn't get out of bed. Rich was out of town. Everyone was busy and couldn't help. Nik was traveling, Cec and Nooch were working. Marc volunteered to pick Aiden up at daycare for me and bring him home. I had to call the preschool to let them know someone else coming to pick up Aiden.

"So his name is Marc. Aiden knows him. It's fine for him to go with him in the car."

"Got it," the school director said.

"Oh, and you're welcome," I said.

Twenty minutes later, after Marc picked Aiden up from school, the director called me.

"Hot damn! Now I know why you said 'You're welcome.' That guy is hot!"

Nicole and Marc live life differently than I do. Marc and Nicole are late night, party people. Their lives are like polar opposites of mine. I'm waking up when they're just getting home. I'm a day person, they're night owls. I was on a schedule to get married, have kids, and settle down. Nicole never settled. And thank goodness because if she settled she never would have found Marc, who is wonderful. Nicole is a spontaneous, fly by the seat of her pants kind of girl. If I called her right now and said, "Let's fly to Paris and go crazy!" She would, one, say yes in a heartbeat. And two, know that something was wrong because I'm a planner and would never do that.

One time, Richard was out of town, and my house alarm went off in the middle of the night. That shit is so fucking loud! I was so scared! My son managed to stay asleep. I don't know how he was able to do that. My heart was racing.

"Hello?" I answered my cell phone. I don't get great service at my house because we live on a hilltop in a mountainous area of Los Angeles.

"Yes, Ma'am. Would you like me to cancel the fire department from coming? Is this a false alarm?"

What kind of Alarm Company assumes it's a false alarm? Shouldn't they always assume there's an emergency? All hands on deck! I mean, really.

"No! My husband is out of town and I have no clue why it's going off. Please send me help." I was panicked. My house phone line wasn't working and I had my cell phone high in the air to keep the signal. I was convinced some burglars that wanted to kill me had cut my house phone line. I watched too many Soap Operas as a teenager. That's what happens when something bad is about to happen … the phone lines are cut. Cue the organ music.

The fire department showed up. It turned out my stupid batteries were dying, and it set off the alarm detecting a fire that wasn't even occurring. They changed the battery in my alarm and fire detector.

"All fixed now Miss. You'll be fine."

"Wait!" I shouted after them as they were walking towards my front door. "Please don't go. I am so scared and I don't think I'll be able to fall back asleep."

"Don't you have anyone you can call? I know it's three in the morning, but maybe a family member or friend?"

A light bulb went off. "Yes! Yes, I do. Thank you gentleman." I ran back to my room after locking up and setting the wretched house alarm. I picked up the phone, hid under the covers, and called Panooch. She answered on the second ring.

"G? What's going on?"

I explained what happened and told her how scared I was to go back to bed. "Do you want me to come over there?"

"No, don't be silly. I have to get ready for work in a couple hours. Can you just talk to me?" And she did. Nicole stayed on the phone with me until 4:15 in the morning. I don't think we said goodbye. I think I fell asleep while she talked to me about her night out. Her voice calmed me like a mom soothing her frightened child. This was what life was like for me. I didn't have much family out in LA but I had my girls. I always knew I could count on them at any given time. And I would always be there for them.

A few weeks later, Rich was working on a show at the Hollywood Bowl honoring President Clinton's birthday and the ten-year anniversary of his foundation. It was a star-studded event and had a huge line up of performances by Stevie Wonder, Usher, Lady Gaga, and many other performers from around the world. Whenever I get tickets to an event from my husband, I rotate between my three girls. I've taken Nikki to the Oscars and Stand Up to Cancer; I've taken Panooch to CNN Heroes and the Emmy's. Cec has come with me to a Divas concert and album release parties. It was Panooch's turn for this one and she was so bummed she couldn't go. She had to work and couldn't get her shift at the bar covered. Her husband, Marc, wanted to go with me, though. Marc: gorgeous, lovable Brit, with a heart of gold, and so much fun to be with.

"Sure I'll hang out with your hot as hell hubby!"

When Marc and Nicole were getting married in Italy, no one was invited. They just wanted it to be them over a cliff off the Mediterranean, pledging their love for one another. However, my husband and I were their witnesses at the Italian Consulate for the marriage license, so at least we got to be a part of their big day in a small way.

So, Marc and I went out to dinner first. We went to a sushi restaurant by their place because you can walk to the Bowl from where they live in Hollywood. Panooch gave him strict instructions not to let me drink too much. Remember my bachelorette party?

We had some sake and then one glass of wine. I was feeling buzzed but not drunk and was just ready for a great time at the concert. As we were leaving the restaurant we planned on buying a bottle of wine to have at the show. We bought a nice $40 bottle of Pinot Grigio, which was perfect on a hot night in the middle of summer. As we were walking up the hill, we saw signs that said, "No glass, No cans." That's weird. You can bring wine into the Hollywood Bowl. Apparently you can't do that all of the time.

"Shit! We just spent $40 on a bottle of wine, and we were going to have to throw it away!"

Marc looked at me as we approached the line for security. The guards would make us throw it away as soon as we got to the metal detector. He raised his eyebrow as if to suggest something naughty. I smiled.

"Let's do it."

We uncorked the bottle and proceeded to down it. Marc kept telling me how proud he was of me and that I was drinking with a Brit, so I'd need to keep up. We finished the bottle and threw it away just as we approached the security station. I was feeling uncertain of my footing. My head was spinning and I kept laughing. People around us were laughing at us. My husband was texting me to let me know the show was starting late because security was taking a long time.

"Rich said they're holding the show because security is so backed up. It's because of those two drunk, crazy people downing a bottle of wine that's making it take long!"

Finally, we went to our seats. We were giggling like schoolgirls because the show was about to start, oh, and we were piss ass drunk. Stevie Wonder opened the show. It was amazing. Marc and I were dancing and singing. Marc knew every word of his songs, which impressed my drunken self. When it was over, another performer came on that we didn't know. Marc decided to go to the bathroom. When he came back, he had a beer in his hand and a huge cup of sangria. No, huge doesn't describe it. It was a fucking bottle of wine in a cup the length of my arm!

"Turns out you can drink at this thing!" Marc shouted.

I looked at Marc like he had two heads. Maybe he did. Sure looked that way from all the other alcohol in my system. Was he crazy? There was no way I could drink that and still stand up.

"I'll help. Just enjoy yourself."

Soooooo … we finished the damn thing and I don't think I could feel my face. After Usher performed, I had to go pee. I assured Marc that I could go by myself, even though I was wobble-walking like I just turned one-year-old, and just learning to take my first steps.

Thankfully, I made it to the restroom. I washed my hands, splashed some water on my face, and was ready to go back to my seat. I needed to sober up!

When I was walking back, I realized I had no idea where we were sitting. I tried to scan my brain for any memory of where our seats were. I couldn't remember a thing. I was questioning my own name at that point. Section K? "Why is this place so big?" I thought to myself. Maybe I said it out loud. I don't know.

I walked up a couple of steps and decided to sit down and text Marc. The cell service at the Bowl is terrible, so I was waiting for the text to go through.

"Sweetie, are you ok?"

It was a nice, older man, who looked like my dad. It wasn't my dad, but he was built the same way and looked about the same age.

"Daddy!" I don't think I said it out loud, but one can never be too sure.

I felt comfortable talking to him. "Oh, I'm fine. I'm just looking for my friend. I can't remember where our seats are."

It was then that I realized that it was warm where I was sitting. Why is this chair so warm? Oh, that's not a chair, that's this stranger's lap! I was sitting in this guy's lap! I turned my head, looked to my right, and saw Marc doubled over, laughing hysterically. He had seen the whole thing go down. "Drunk Jen" wandering in the aisles and randomly sitting on some sixty five-year-old's lap. I was mortified! And I was only one section away from my seat.

Marc came over to the man.

"Sorry mate," He said as he scooped me up off the guy's lap.

He brought me back to our seats. I wish I could tell you the guy's reaction. I don't remember it. I do remember Marc saying, "I better tell Rich." He then texted Rich. The text was Marc groveling for forgiveness.

Marc: I am so sorry, man. I might have gotten Jen a little drunk.

Rich: A little? I know what that means. She's your problem now, Buddy.

He had been warned. Now he knows not to let me get so intoxicated. Lesson learned. Now what?

We got back to Panooch's apartment. I laid down on the futon. It was the futon I had in my apartment when I first moved to town. Panooch wanted it when I moved in with Rich. It was like sleeping in my 20's all over again. Panooch got home from work and yelled at Marc for not listening to her about pacing my drinking. I passed out and when I woke up, raging headache and all, I went home. Thankfully, Rich got home earlier and sent the babysitter home. That would have been expensive!

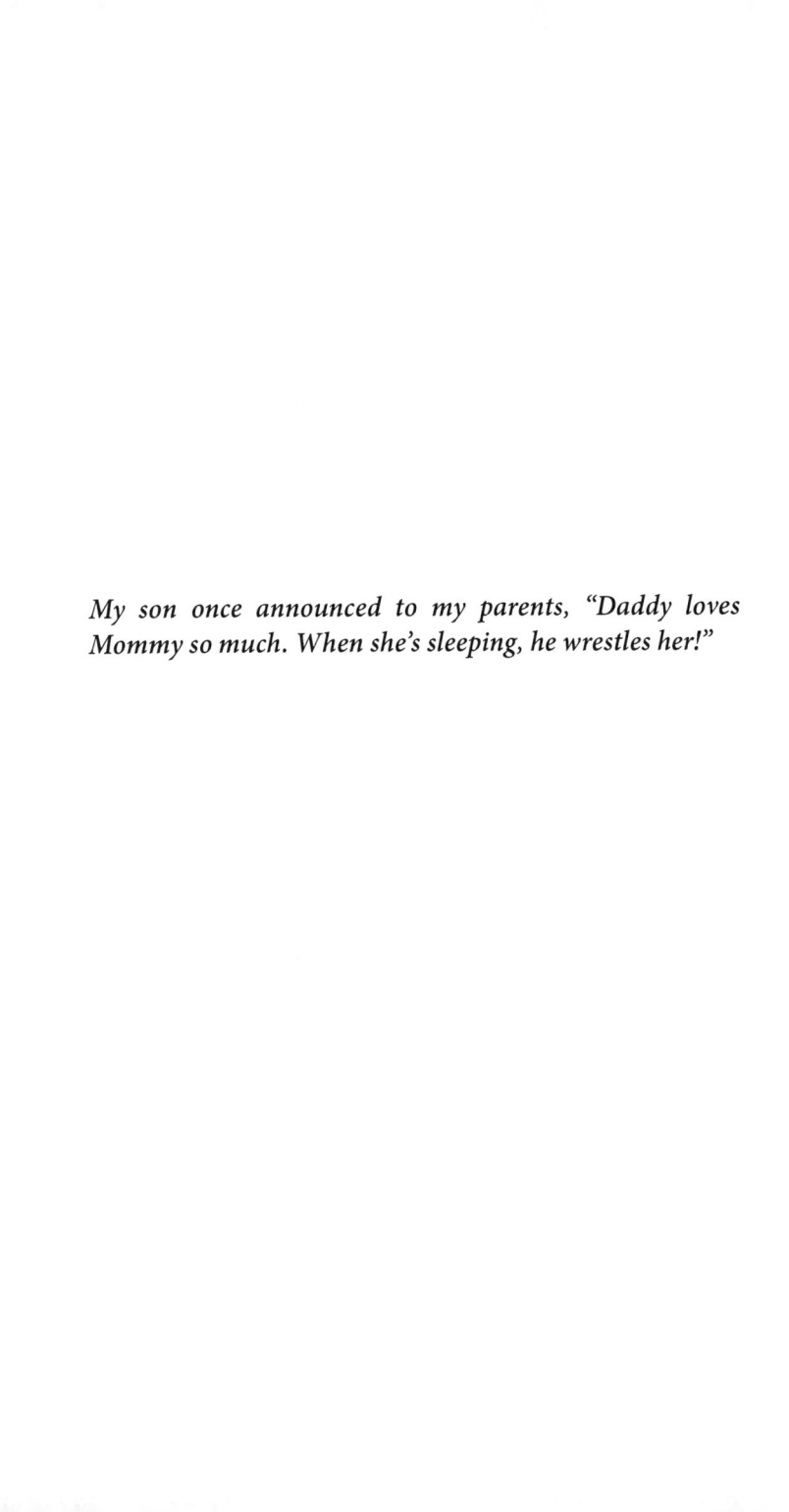

My son once announced to my parents, "Daddy loves Mommy so much. When she's sleeping, he wrestles her!"

Chapter Nine

After I had my daughter Jocelyn Nicole—named for Nicole who watched Aiden while I was at the hospital delivering his sister—I had a touch of postpartum depression. By touch, I mean I suffered from postpartum depression. My mom called it "Baby Blues." I think she was afraid of the label. All I knew was; I cried most of the time, didn't want to play with the kids, hated being back at work, and daydreamed of running away.

My doctor gave me the medical intervention, as I like to call it. It got me out of bed and stopped me from crying, no more thoughts of running away, and I was once again the "Hide and Seek Queen!"

But I couldn't cry. It didn't matter what it was; I couldn't cry.

Heard of someone that died. Nothing.

Watched the hospital scene from *Terms of Endearment*. Dry as the desert.

Saw an Oprah episode that reunited a soldier and his family after three years of deployment. Blank stare.

Slammed my hand in the door when I was trying to not let the door close before grabbing my purse. Sure, there were major curse words, screaming, stomping up and down. But the driest eyes in the west.

I hadn't cried in six months! It was so unlike me.

Rich decided I needed a "Mom Weekend" away. He got me a room at a nice hotel and made sure it was near Nikki so she could hang with me if I decided I wanted company. He also gave me a DVD player and a documentary he thought I would like.

So, armed with my movie and PJ's, I was ready for a relaxing weekend.

My first night I took a hot bath and had Rich on the speakerphone the whole time.

"You know you could be doing this at home?"

"I know, but I like talking to you."

"Call me if you can't sleep. Love you."

"Good night."

I sat in the tub until I was a prune. I wrapped myself in a towel, looked at the clock and saw it was only 9 p.m. I took an Ambien and was knocked out cold.

Nikki came over in the morning around 9 a.m. She got in bed with me and we talked. Some of my best memories with Nik are just lying around talking.

"So how are you feeling? Really? Not the answer everyone wants to hear. How are you *really* doing?"

"I'm OK, I guess. I feel fine. I just can't cry. It's not like me."

We decided to watch the movie Rich sent for me to watch. He said it was so good, but intense. He said I had to watch it!

The movie was called *Dear Zachary: A Letter to a Son About His Father*. I don't want to ruin this for you but am going to have to if you want to understand the full scope of this story with Nikki. So if you have interest in watching this documentary, which is a great film, please, I won't be offended, skip ahead and read the next chapter.

In a nutshell, the movie was made by a man's best friend's son. The boy's father was murdered and his best friend wanted the boy to get to know his father. The father's ex-girlfriend, who is the boy's mother, and murdered the boy's father. The father's parents had custody of the baby for the first year because the mother was in jail. At some point the mother got out and had visitation rights and would visit with the baby. At the end of the documentary, it's revealed that the baby is dead! That's right. Dead! The mother jumped in a lake with the baby strapped to her along with a ton of bricks (or something that made them sink to the bottom). Uplifting, right? So this guy made this documentary about his best friend so his best friend's kid would know about his father. The kid will never see the movie made for him because his mother committed a suicide/murder.

Nikki was a fucking mess. She was sobbing into the pillow as we lay on our side watching the end credits roll. Now, the end of this film shocked me, don't get me wrong. It is a horrific incident and another example of how we need to look at mental health in this country. However, was this the best movie my husband could have sent me off to watch on my "Sorry You Have Postpartum Depression Weekend, Here's a Break?" I think not! Nikki looked at me like I was insane.

"Really? Not even that gets a tear?"

"I got nothing."

"I can't believe Rich sent that for you to watch this weekend. Do you think he wanted to help get you to cry?"

"I don't know. I don't think he's that in touch with what's going on with me. He probably likes that I can't cry."

"Maybe he wanted you to see there are crazier people out there than you?" "Knowing Rich, he saw it, was moved by it, and wanted to share, not thinking of the content not being the best for my 'Mom's weekend.'"

On any other given day or circumstance, I can't imagine a time when anyone would want to watch something so sad. Don't get me wrong. It's an important story to tell. It's just not the kind of movie that you say, "You know what I want to watch? I want to watch a movie that will depress me as I watch a family lose not one but two important people to them. One of which is a baby who never got a chance to live his life! Oh and it's because his mother killed his father and the baby—heartwarming!"

A couple weeks later, Rich was out of town. I took the kids to the mall for some shopping and quite frankly, something to do. When my kids were little, I never knew what to do for entertainment. I didn't enjoy that part. I had my friends and didn't need to bond with strangers just because we had kids that were born around the same time.

I had a hard time getting the stroller out of the trunk. After wrestling with the stupid double stroller, I got it out after banging my hand against the car really hard. Again, there were no tears.

I went into the mall and we went straight to the food court. I got the kids their food and sat down. Some creepy guy sat next to us and started talking to me. I remember looking down at my hand to make sure he saw that I was married and to stop being creepy. That's a good strategy. Hey I'm married … no creepy guy here, please.

He eventually went away. The kids and I went about our usual visits to run around the Disney store, get a free sample from See's Candy, and play on the mall rides.

I saw a sign for a sale at Macy's and decided to try a couple things on. The kids were behaving and I figured I was on borrowed time. I tried a shirt on and when I saw it fit, I tried to take it off so I could buy it. No telling how long the kids were going to keep behaving. While taking the shirt off, it got stuck on something. Freeing myself, I noticed that the shirt was stuck on my ring! My center diamond had fallen out somehow and the prongs stuck to the shirt! Frantic, I began to search all the clothing in the dressing room. I made my kids get out of the stroller as I searched it. I ran through the department store, retracing my steps. We ran through See's, the Disney Store, and the Food Court. And nothing! My two-carat, beautiful engagement stone was gone! GONE! My heart was racing, my palms were sweaty, and I started to hyperventilate. It was then that I realized: I was crying! It started down my cheek, as I realized, my stone was gone forever. Someone would find it and think it was glass. It was to get swept up and thrown in the trash. A diamond, worth $8,000, was going to be trash! The night he proposed was etched in my mind. It was one of my most treasured memories. I remembered that beautiful evening every time I looked at my left hand. I remember thinking when Rich gave it to me, "Oh my God. That is exactly what I wanted! That ring is beyond beautiful!" As I thought these things, the tears came faster and faster. How was I going to tell Rich?

I called Nikki. "Hooray! You're crying! That's great!"

I choked on my words as I said, "Yeah, terrific. Now I can't *stop* crying!"

"Relax, Jen. Just call your insurance company and make a claim. That way Rich will be sad but know it can be replaced."

Cut to me calling the insurance company and finding out that my policy lapsed when we moved, and I forgot to change the address, and I was no longer insured for my ring! No problem crying anymore. As a matter of fact, hysteria set in. I can still hear Nikki putting my ass in check.

"Jen!" —In her authoritative, no-nonsense, you're being an asshole voice— "It's a stone. Not a life. Things can be replaced. Get over yourself. Yes, be upset, I get it. In the long run, you are going to survive."

Postpartum depression taught me a lot. I am grateful it's over and grateful for the stories and lessons that came out of it. No problem crying anymore. My emotions are fully in check. Maybe I should re-watch that movie.

You're dead to me ...

Chapter Ten

Like all relationships, things weren't always perfect. In 2008, Chris and Cec were supposed to come to our house for Thanksgiving. That time of year is hard for me. All of my family lives back East, and I hate missing Thanksgiving with them. It was too expensive to fly there for just four days. The time change was hard for the kids (who were so young at the time). I was sad to miss cooking with my mom and brothers for the holiday. It was important to me that I create some traditions out here that I could count on. If I couldn't be with my family, then I could be with my best friends that feel like family. The year before, we spent the holiday at our house with Cecilia, Chris, her parents and brother and our great friends Michael and David. We had a blast. I couldn't wait to have a wonderful memory again. I called Cec a couple of times leading up to Thanksgiving.

"Hey Cec. It's Jen. I wanted to see how many people were coming next Thursday for Thanksgiving?"

Cecilia never answered my calls or returned my messages. I got frustrated.

"Cec. I haven't heard from you and I am starting to get worried. Please call me back."

She still never called. So I tried Chris.

"Chris. It's Jen. What is going on? I left Cec a bunch of messages. Are you guys coming to Thanksgiving or not?"

What was going on? At this point I wasn't worried that something bad had happened. I was just so mad they weren't calling me back.

Thanksgiving came and went. We just had the holiday by ourselves. I know I should have been grateful to have my husband and kids but holidays, for me, have always been lots of people around. Who would tell me what a great cook I was if it was just the four of us? My husband and kids have my cooking every day. I needed the crowd to give me my ego boost.

Cecilia's mom left me a message days later apologizing for not calling sooner and saying she was sorry they couldn't make it this year. But never anything from Cecilia or Chris.

Time went by. Days turned into weeks and weeks into months.

So there it was: this friendship that I thought was my whole world—and it was over! Because of turkey! I didn't understand why? Had I done something wrong? Was I too pushy in trying to recreate the year before? Why was this happening?

Two years went by with no word! Well, Cecilia called me on my son's birthday in April, and I didn't answer. I was too hurt. I remember we were at Disneyland, celebrating, and I looked at my phone and saw it was Cec. You know that feeling when your heart feels like it's in your stomach? That's what I was feeling.

Then anger took over. I showed Rich who was calling, and before he could tell me to answer, I said, "Maybe she's calling to say she's not coming to Thanksgiving." And I threw my phone back in the backpack.

But one Saturday in 2010, my housekeeper, Maria, came over and changed my life forever.

The day I showed up at Cecilia's was the day Chris was being transferred to USC Hospital. This hospital specialized in Leukemia. Chris had AML (Acute Myeloid Leukemia).

After the shock of seeing me on her doorstep, and clearing up how I was able to get into the complex so easily, we started to talk.

"I don't understand. How can he have cancer?"

"He was having these stomach problems. Remember when he used to get stomach aches and throw up?"

I nodded. Chris would go through these periods where he would feel sick and end up making himself throw up just to get rid of the nausea. It started out once in a while. Maybe it happened one time while we worked together. I noticed it more when he went to another school and around the time he and Cecilia got married. I thought maybe he had Irritable Bowel Syndrome but remembered they had that checked out by their doctor.

"It got bad. I'd get home from work; he'd be in the bathroom, sick as a dog. He'd yell at me and take out his irritations on me, and I just thought he was being a jerk. He wouldn't let me help him, even though his usual coping mechanisms weren't working. I put my foot down and made him go to the hospital late on last

Friday night. Cami was at my parents for the night, and I sat in the ER with Chris for hours. When the doctor saw him, he said it was one of two things. He either had a rare stomach condition or leukemia."

At this point in her story, Cecilia and I were holding hands. I was rubbing the back of her hand and encouraged her to continue.

"I thought, 'Finally! We're going to get answers.' Because, obviously, he doesn't have cancer, right?"

"Oh my God." That's all I could say. I was in denial like maybe this story was going to end with him having a stomach condition and he would be fine.

"But then the results came back. It's Cancer. And can you believe it? They are sending him to USC today for some experimental treatment." She said this like it was the most disgusting part of the story.

Chris was a die-hard UCLA fan. As far as he was concerned, Trojans were only good for one thing. Being at a USC hospital was going to be torture, but not as torturous as the road that was ahead of him.

I just sat on her couch, holding her hand, listening. I didn't know what to do. But sitting there in Chris and Cecilia's house for the first time in so long, holding my best friend's hand as she told me the worst news she would ever tell me, I knew that I was where I was meant to be. And it forced me to reflect on the kind of friend I had been and on the kind of friend I wanted to be in the future.

No amount of time or silly arguments could ever break us apart. She was part of me, and I was part of her. Cecilia is in my blood, my brain, my heart, and my soul. This tragedy of Chris getting sick was a wakeup call for me. It was a good slap in the face to remind me of what is important in life. Cecilia and I would never be apart again.

Chris went through months of agonizing testing and treatments. We thought the nightmare was over when he got a bone marrow transplant with 99.9% match but a month later the doctor called and gave the bad news that it didn't work. It was too late. His body had too many cancer cells. He was given one month to live.

I'll never forget the morning I was going to see him in the hospital. I remember saying to Rich that I didn't know when I would be home, but I would try to get back to help with the kids and do the laundry.

"You're being ridiculous right now. Spend as much time as you need with Chris. It could be the last."

Those words stuck in the air like gasoline stays in your nose after smelling it. I drove over to pick Cecilia up and drive together to the hospital. When we got to the hospital, Cecilia gave Chris and me some time alone. She needed to talk to his doctor and wanted us to be able to have some time together. He was so heavily drugged. Bald head, lost look in his eyes. This was not the Chris that I used to tease about eating radishes like apples and having his mother pack his lunches for him at the age of twenty-four. I tried not to get emotional, but as soon as I started speaking, I was a sobbing mess.

"I'm so sorry you have to go through this." He just

stared at me. His reactions were delayed, and slurred speech made it difficult to understand him when he did try to talk.

I shouldn't have cried in front of him. I didn't want to make him feel uncomfortable or feel the need to comfort me. But this just wasn't my Chris. Chris teased me or challenged me. We never ran out of things to talk about.

I broke the uncomfortable silence after a few minutes.

"Can I get you anything or do anything to make you feel more comfortable?"

We were sitting across from one another in the hospital chairs.

"Yeah ... lift ... your ... leg." He said in a drugged voice.

Hmm.

So I lifted my leg and then was unsure why he wanted me to do that.

"Now what?" I asked. He smirked ever so slightly and said, "You ... can ... put ... it ... down ... now."

We spent a couple of hours together. We went for a walk. I pushed him in his wheelchair and told him about work. It ended up being a lovely day together, even though he was out of it. Borrowed time. Stolen moments. This is what it came down to in those last few months.

Later, the following week, Chris went home and was off a lot of the medicine, he was getting back to his usual personality. He could speak clearly, move faster, and aside from the disgusting cancer traveling in his blood, he was back to his usual self, for the most part. Cec and I asked him if he remembered the day I visited him at the hospital. He said he did. I just had to know.

"Why did you want me to lift my leg?"

He smiled at me, and in a matter of fact voice said, "I wanted to see if you'd do it."

We all cracked up laughing. Thank God he still had his sense of humor in the midst of hell.

The following week, Rich and I decided to make Chris one of his favorite meals: pulled pork sandwiches, coleslaw, BBQ potato chips, and pecan pie. I wanted to make him a homemade pecan pie. I was in a rush, as usual, and had to use store bought crust, though. It burned around some of the edges, and I was so upset. Of course, I had to let everyone know how upset I was about my pie crust and that I DID NOT make the crust!

Chris just ate it and said, "Jen, you sure make great pecan pie filling!"

That was Chris, always quietly making fun of me.

Cecilia decided to start a diary for the New Year.

She began her first entry like this: "Dear Diary, wait. Is that what I'm supposed to say? I'm 36!"

And that was the end of her New Year's Diary.

Chapter Eleven

WE WERE ALL SO relieved when Chris was able to make it to Cami's fifth birthday. He was starting to have a persistent cough. I remember him needing to go in the house to lie down after Camille blew out her candles on her cake. I also remember thinking, "This is going to be their last family picture." The thought devastated me.

On February 6, 2011, Cecilia called me and told me Chris had pneumonia, and the doctor said it was the turn for the worse we all feared. I went straight to the hospital after work. Thankfully, Rich was home and could take care of the kids. When I got to the hospital, Chris's parents were there. I felt compelled to say something to Chris's mom. After all, she was losing her son. I couldn't ever imagine what that was like. I went over to her, hugged her, and told her how sorry I was. We talked for a few minutes and then she and her husband went to get something to eat while I went in to visit with Chris. I walked in, trying to have a smile on my face, but knowing this was it. It was time to say goodbye. It just felt wrong. It didn't feel real. At any moment, they'd call cut, and it would all have just been a dramatic Lifetime television movie. Except it wasn't a movie, it was real life, and we were the dramatic actors playing the roles of "grown-ups." Don't old people say goodbye to their friends? Not thirty-five-year-olds.

The doctor came in to explain that the pneumonia had been too much for Chris's body to fight off and the best thing to do would be to keep him comfortable from now on. Blood transfusions and platelets each week had prolonged his life up to this point, but his body was too sick and weak to fight off the infection. Chris looked at the doctor as he suggested going on Hospice. He looked like the doctor just told him he was going to lose a baseball game, no matter how many times he hit the ball out of the park.

A woman who worked at the hospital came in minutes later to discuss how hospice worked. Maybe I should have excused myself at this point, but I didn't. I just stood there, frozen in place, wishing this were all a lie.

"I don't want to feel like I am giving up," Chris told her. I'll never get her voice out of my head. Her response was astonishing.

"Well, there's always hope," she said.

What?!? Hope!? Fuck you lady! That's what I wanted to scream. Don't tell my dying friend there's always hope! All that I kept thinking about was how he was going to miss watching his beautiful daughter grow up and how we would never get to teach at the same school again, and how Cecilia was going to somehow have to pick up the pieces of her shattered life. That lady can take her hope and shove it up her ass. Who taught her how to speak to dying people like that, because she failed. Fuck that. I needed to get out of there. I excused myself and went to the bathroom.

Of course, the door was locked and someone was using the bathroom, so I waited, trying to calm down my overactive emotions. I glanced to my right and noticed a wall full of pamphlets about Cancer. There was one about treatment. One about pets helping patients heal. One about nutrition and exercise, and one that caught my eye: "How to Be a Friend to Someone with Cancer."

I opened it up and started reading. It said that when visiting a friend with cancer, you should be sure to follow a few simple rules to make the visit successful. Here's what it said:

> » *Always call before visiting. Be understanding if your friend can't see you at that time.*
>
> » *Schedule a visit with the caregiver to provide physical and emotional support. Maybe you can stay with the patient while the caregiver takes a break.*
>
> » *Make short, periodic visits rather than long infrequent ones. Patients might not want to talk, but they may not like being alone either.*
>
> » *Begin and end the visit with a touch, a hug, or a handshake.*
>
> » *Be understanding if the family asks you to leave.*
>
> » *Always refer to your next visit so your friend can look forward to it.*
>
> » *Offer to take a snack or treat to share so your visit doesn't impose on the caregiver.*

> » Try to visit at times other than weekends or holidays, when others may visit. Time can seem the same to a housebound patient. A Tuesday morning can be just as lonely as a Saturday night.
>
> » Take your own needlework, crossword puzzles, or books and keep them company while they chat or doze off to sleep.

Then there's a picture of a woman, who is around seventy years old, in a loving embrace with a man, whose face you do not see, and the woman is smiling. Under the picture, it says, "Don't be afraid to touch, hug, or shake hands with your friend."

I ran back to the hospital room and burst through the door.

"Shit, Chris! I've been doing it all wrong this whole time! If only I had read this pamphlet months ago, I could have been a better "Friend to Someone with Cancer." I tossed the pamphlet on his bed. He picked it up and looked at it for a minute. He grinned his famous grin, looked at me, and said, "You really should have read this before." We all laughed and proceeded to have a dramatic reading of the pamphlet. I acted out each bullet point, and when it said to touch your friend, I placed my hand on Chris's shoulder, looked him in the eye and said, "I forgot to pee. I'll be right back. I want you to know when I'm coming back because that's what a friend to a cancer patient does. They let them know when they will see them again. Be right back."

I went back down the hall with a huge smile on my face. I know it wasn't hope that I gave him, but at least we were able to laugh together in his darkest hours. The bathroom was vacant and I went in. I looked at myself in the mirror and the floodgates opened. Saying goodbye is never easy. I was filled with so much regret for the two years I had missed and all the special times we could have had.

I let myself cry for only a minute. I peed, splashed water on my face, and went back to Chris's room. His parents were back from the cafeteria. They had brought Cecilia and me a menu in case we wanted to see what food was available.

I sat next to Chris and asked him what he thought sounded yummy. He asked me to read the options. Along the side it had a menu of specials by day.

"Chris, you couldn't have been here two days ago? They had chili that day! You know how I love chili."

"I'm sorry. Why don't you try the roasted chicken with gravy and mashed potatoes?" he said. I smiled and we went back and forth about different food on the menu. This led into my making fun, yet again, of how his mom always packed his lunch for him.

"Well, I was packing one for me so I figured I could pack one for him too." She defended herself with a smile on her face. We all shared more stories and laughed a lot that night. Oddly, it was a great night.

When it was time to leave because visiting hours were over, I leaned over to give Chris a kiss on the cheek. I put my hand on his shoulder and looked him in the eye.

"I'll see you tomorrow, my friend."

As I walked to my car that night, I knew it was not

the last time I would see him. I don't know how I knew that, but somehow my heart and brain were working together, telling me it was not the last time.

The next day, Chris was released from the hospital, and a hospital bed was set up in their living room. Chris had developed an eye infection and looked like he had been in a bar fight. He was weak. He wasn't able to get up the stairs easily. The following day it was his birthday and I wanted to see him after work. I had my son, Aiden, with me and we were on our way to pick up my daughter, Jocelyn, from preschool. Aiden and I stopped at the house to say happy birthday. I wasn't sure Chris would be up for a long visit, but I knew Aiden wanted to give him a picture he made for him.

Kid drawings are so brilliant in their simplicity. This picture was of Chris in a hospital bed. When I say "Chris" I mean a stick figure laying on what I assume is a bed. He had the stick figure Chris saying in a speech bubble, "I hope this works." The stick figure doctor was touching stick figure Chris's arm and saying in a speech bubble, "I think it will!"

When we got to the house, I tried to prepare Aiden that Uncle Chris was not going to look like he always did in the past and that we wouldn't stay long so he could rest. When we walked in, Chris was sitting up in his hospital bed.

"Happy birthday, Uncle Chris, I am sorry you're sick." I'll never forget Chris's response.

"Aw thanks, Buddy. Come here." Chris gestured for Aiden to climb up on the bed. He hugged him as tightly as he could. I remember thinking the word gratitude. Gratitude was what I felt for this man at that moment. He could barely move, talking was difficult, his eye was swollen and yet he took the minute to make my son feel loved and special.

Aiden gave Chris the picture he made, and Chris thanked him.

"Let's let Uncle Chris get some rest now," I told Aiden. He hugged Chris one more time and hopped off the bed. I leaned into Chris's side and touched his shoulder for what would be the last time. Remember how I just knew the night before how it wasn't the last time I would see him? This moment felt the same except this time; I *knew* it *was* the last.

"I love you, Chris. Find peace, my friend. Find peace," I whispered in his ear. Those were the last words I ever got to say to my sweet friend. This was my friend who stormed out of my house when he was losing a board game. My friend who came to my rescue the day I swore there was a snake in my house. My friend who used to convince me we had time to run out for lunch with only forty minutes of a lunch break and would get us back to school just as the bell was ringing and I was freaking out over being late. This was my friend who laughed with me no matter where we were—whether it was at work, home, or even in a hospital room.

I said my goodbyes and cried all the way home.

The next night Cecilia called and said the hospice nurse said, "It's happening tonight."

She asked me to call the Neptune Society to arrange everything ahead of time so that if Chris went in the middle of the night, she would know what to do. I made all the arrangements. After calling Cec back to let her know the plan, I went to sleep. There really was nothing else for me to do.

It was 2:00 in the morning when I woke up. I don't know why I woke up but I did. I was staring at the clock and watching the minutes pass when my phone rang. I answered on the first ring.

"It happened," she whispered. A lonely tear rolled down my cheek.

"OK" I whispered. "Do you need me to come over? I can be there in twenty minutes," I offered.

"No, Kevin is here and we have to get Chris ready to be picked up. Come over in the morning," she said.

We hung up. At least Chris's brother was with her. I woke Rich up.

"He's gone!" I wailed. The floodgates had opened. I let all my tears out on his shoulder. He held me for what felt like forever. He suggested I take a hot bath and try to relax before going over to Cec's. He drew me a bath and I laid in the hot water for an hour. After my bath I tried to lie back in bed until it was light enough out to call it morning and head over to Cecilia's and bring her some coffee.

When I got back in my bed I was facing my clock again. I felt a squeeze on my shoulder and thought how sweet Rich was being. He got my bath ready, had held me while I cried, and now was squeezing my shoulder. I rolled over to hug him back and found him sound asleep. He wasn't touching me. I know this sounds crazy, but it gives me comfort because I believe that the feeling I had of being squeezed on my shoulder was Chris saying goodbye. He probably had that smirk on his face too. The one that said, "Gotcha!"

I went over to Cecilia's around six in the morning, and a couple of other girlfriends from work were already there. We started making plans for Chris's memorial service. Cec and Chris met in high school and were together for eighteen years! There were so many people to notify and so much to do.

"Do you think Nikki and Tommy can sing at the service?"

"I'm sure they'd be honored," I replied.

After Nikki got divorced, she met her true love, Tommy. He is an amazing musician and a great friend to all of us. Nikki is an incredible singer too. Having them at the service was also soothing for me. I was trying to be strong for Cecilia, Nikki was there for me. That's what gets us through times like these.

Camille had gone to her grandmother's house and came back in the late morning. I sat with her on the couch and read her my favorite childhood book: *Alexander and the Terrible, Horrible, No Good, Very Bad Day*. Chris had given me the twenty-seventh edition on my twenty-seventh birthday, and it was a special copy. He was mad at me when I wrote my name on the inside of it because I just devalued the book. Teachers have to write their names on their book! It's our thing. Besides, I would never sell that book! Every time I read it to my first graders I tell them a special person gave it to me.

When I finished reading to Camille, I left so Cecilia and she could have some time to process things together. When I left, the song *"My Life Would Suck Without You"* came on the radio. It was like Kelly Clarkson wrote the story of Cecilia's and my friendship. My life would suck without Cecilia. I thank Chris everyday for giving her to me.

Cecilia was doing homework with Camille.

Camille said, "Mommy, I want to be just like you when I grow up."

Cecilia responded with a stern voice, "You will NOT be like me when you grow up!"

Chapter Twelve

"I NEED TO SEE CHRIS one more time!"

Cec called me one morning and was going on and on about visiting Chris. We were in the middle of planning his funeral service. Nikki and Tommy were set to sing at the service. Panooch and Marc were out of town in England visiting his family.

We were planning to have the service in the auditorium of the last school Chris worked at. It was extremely emotional planning the service, but we wanted to honor him the best way we knew how. So at first I thought Cecilia was delusional, talking about visiting Chris.

"Cec, he died, remember? You can't visit him. He's at the crematorium, not the hospital."

"I know. But you can pay extra money to have a viewing of the body one more time. Jen, I need to do this. If this was me, I know he would come see me one more time. This is the last time I'll get to say 'I'm going to see Chris.'"

"How much is it?"

"Four hundred dollars."

"Ok. That's a lot of money. You're sure you want to do this?"

"I need to do this. But I can't do it alone."
"Obviously I'm coming with you."
"Thank God."

So I guess I was taking the day off to go "visit Chris." That sounded so crazy to say. It felt like he wasn't gone. It's moments like this you realize when we say "visit" him, it won't be him anymore. The service was planned for Sunday. Nikki and Tommy's music was being rehearsed, food was ordered, slide show prepared. Now all we had to do was go see Chris one more time before they cremated him. We'll add it to the checklist.

Most people think it's morbid that I went with Cecilia to see Chris's body before he was cremated. I didn't look at it that way. Chris wanted to be cremated. Cecilia also invited Chris's parents and brother to the viewing. I went because I was doing it for Cecilia and I loved Chris. Sure it wasn't the best way to spend a day. I certainly would rather tell you a story about when we went to Palm Springs and stayed in bed the whole time re-watching The Notebook five times after finding hot, sexy, deleted scenes on YouTube. But this is real life. Life isn't full of all funny and happy stories. The moments we struggle through the most are the ones that shape us to face the future. It's moments like these that also solidify my bond with this woman. I would do anything for Cecilia, and I know she would do anything for me. Besides, with Cecilia and me, there is always something funny and silly that happens, even in a sad story.

I didn't care that we were going to see Chris dead in a box. That doesn't gross me out. After Cec called

I knew I wanted to hold his hand one last time and I knew Cecilia couldn't do this by herself. The drive alone was a nostalgic one.

"We're going to see Chris. This will be the last time we get to say that." Cecilia was pensive and stoic on the drive there.

We were meeting Chris's parents there. I couldn't even begin to imagine what this was like for them. It's not supposed to happen this way. We are supposed to go before our kids.

After driving an hour, we got to the place. I parked the car.

"Oh my God, Jen, where did I send him?"

It was this rundown warehouse on the outskirts of downtown. Honestly, it looked like a crack house. Cecilia was going crazy seeing where it was that Chris's body had been for a week before the cremation.

"That's it! We're breaking him out of here!"

"'Because that wouldn't be insane!' The two of us carrying Chris's dead body out of this place to take him … where exactly?"

After taking a few deep breaths, we decided to go in and meet with the people that we made the appointment with.

Don't judge a book by its cover, though because when went in, the people who worked there were lovely and so sympathetic. After signing some paperwork, we were led to a waiting room, and as we were waiting, Cecilia started worrying that they put the wrong body in the "viewing room." Can you imagine walking into a room, getting the courage to say goodbye to a loved one and it's some other body? That image in my head had me laughing a little too loudly. The man who worked there assured us it was Chris. He told us he was wearing his Bruins shirt and pajama pants, the outfit Chris's brother and Cecilia put him in after he passed. When the guy said what Chris was wearing, I saw Cecilia relax.

We let Chris's parents go first. They spent a few minutes in there. I'll never forget Chris's mom when she came out.

"He looks good," she said.

I don't know what I was thinking. Maybe I'd go in, and Chris would be standing there ready to go out to the movies or something?

Next, it was Chris's brother's turn. A few minutes later, he came out and hugged his parents.

Cecilia was ready to go in. She turned to me.

"I can do this. I'll come get you if I need you."

She turned the doorknob, poked her head around the door and turned back at me.

"Nope! You're coming. I can't do this by myself."

I laughed and just reached out my hand for hers.

We held hands and walked in together. It looked like the longest room ever. It was like an elongated mirrored room in a funhouse. It seemed like it took us fifteen minutes to walk down the hall.

Chris was in a cardboard box which was draped with some makeshift tablecloth. I don't know what we expected. She didn't buy a coffin because he was being cremated, but it was weird to see him in this box. He was not ready to go to the movies; I'll tell you that.

He *was* wearing his UCLA pajamas. And it was indeed Chris.

We started talking to him, and it was the only time I have seen Cecilia cry, still to this day, over the loss of him. I knew this moment was monumental. She keeps everything in, hides behind jokes, and suffers silently. For just these fifteen minutes, she allowed herself to cry unapologetically. I ached for her. I was proud of her. I wished I could take all the pain away.

She was upset how cold he was because he hated being cold and he didn't have socks on. We hugged each other and kissed Chris's hands and cheeks, and we talked to him.

"Say what you need to say, Cecilia. Say what you came here to say."

Through sobs, Cecilia said, "Hi, Babe. I want you to know that Camille and I will be ok. And we'll never forget you."

As she stroked his cheek with the back of her hand she made promises, "I'll do my best to help with her homework. But that was supposed to be your thing since you know how much I hate school."

Then she abruptly yelled, "I promise not to let Camille watch *The Walking Dead* or any other bad things … it was just the one time!"

We laughed.

"He would be rolling his eyes at you if he could right now," I said.

And then it happened! We saw his chest move!

Obviously, it was our eyes playing tricks on us, but we both were so freaked out.

"Did you see that?" Cecilia said

"Yeah, if by 'see that' you mean he just moved!" I yelled.

We huddled together like little girls watching a scary movie and then burst into laughter.

We were able to leave the room with a smile. Just before we opened the door to exit, I pulled Cecilia into my arms.

"I am so proud of you. You are stronger than you give yourself credit for." She was so graceful and mature during this entire process, and she let herself have this cathartic moment. I am so honored I got to share this with her.

After leaving the crematorium (I like saying that word for some reason. I think some guy that I knew that was a stand-up comic had it in a joke that always made me laugh.), we all went to Chris's favorite burger place, The Apple Pan. We all ordered Chris's favorite: hickory burger, extra sauce, crispy fries, and extra sauce for the fries, and then pie. I had pecan pie, and the crust was much better than mine.

My microwave broke. I had to carry this ridiculously heavy thing to Sears because my husband was convinced we had the extended warranty on it. So after a long day at work and two over-stimulated children in tow, I hauled the microwave to the store. I carried the microwave; Aiden carried the glass plate that spins inside it. Jocelyn held onto my arm. No one offered to hold a door for us.

When we got in the store, I asked where I go to check the warranty. Obviously struggling, and not one person offered for me to put the damn thing down or carry it for me! Aiden and Joss saw the TV department on the way to where we were lugging the stupid microwave. In their excitement, over God knows what, Aiden tripped, dropped the glass plate, and it shattered everywhere. Guess that's what Sears gets for not helping me carry the thing in the first place!

Chapter Thirteen

MY MORNINGS ARE INSANE. Once we get out the door, we have forty-five minutes to drive to school/work. My kids go to the school where I teach. Thankfully I have a DVD player in my car and they eat their breakfast while watching Grease for the hundredth time. Every morning I call Cec to check on her. We called it "Coffee Talk."

"Morning," I said in my sing-songy voice.

"Yeah, Hi. So you won't believe the night I had."

She launched into her story ...

"I was driving home from work. I was late picking up Camille, as usual, tired, and hungry. All of a sudden my car started making a weird sound, and I realized I got a flat tire."

"Are you fucking kidding me?" How much more could a person take?

"Oh, I kid you not. I pulled over and picked up the phone and guess who I called?

"Who?"

"Chris!"

My heart sank in my stomach. "Oh my God, Cec. What did you do?"

"The voicemail picked up, so I left him a message."

"You didn't." I don't know how she was keeping it together. My heart was racing hearing the story. She lived it. Yesterday!

"So this is what I said. 'Hey, Babe. It's me. SOOOOO I just got a flat tire, and I'm late picking up Cami. I really wish you were here to help me with either of these things. Except you can't because you're dead!'"

"Cec," I said nervously laughing. "You did not say that!"

"Yeah, I did. And then I told him I didn't think I could do this by myself and then cut myself off apologizing for putting all this on him! Then while I was laughing at my ridiculous message, the voicemail cut me off and said 'Sorry. This voicemail box you are calling is now full. Please call back later.'"

Cecilia just laughed at herself and continued, "Really? This is my life? Ugh."

It's stories like these where you get the essence of who Cecilia is. She is not one to ask for help. She is a private person. She finds those moments to laugh at herself and somehow gets through life appearing not a bit frazzled.

"Yeah, so that happened!" Cecilia said in her jokey/sarcastic tone.

"So what did you end up doing?"

"I called my brother. He picked Cami up and then came and got me. It's fine. Really. I'm fine." She tried to brush it off as if it was nothing.

"Cec. When are you going to be ready to turn that phone off? You can't keep putting yourself through this. How many messages have you left him?"

"Not a lot. I'm just not ready," she said. "It's his phone."

I started to hear her moving fast around her house.

"Ugh, where is Camille? We're going to be late. Camille? Camille, do you have socks on your feet?"

I heard some doors opening and then Camille's voice. Everything sounded muffled like she was hiding the phone under her shirt or something. When she got back on the phone, she sounded winded as she started to talk.

"I just found her in her closet. Before I could ask her what she was doing, she yelled at me that she was talking to Daddy."

"Oh my God. What did you say? I couldn't hear it all."

"I said 'tell him I say hi' and ran out of the room really fast."

"Cec, you need to get her counseling."

"I know. It's on my list. I'm gonna do it."

A few weeks later, while we were talking on my way to work, her home phone rang. She answered it, and the caller asked for Chris. It was a school asking if he could come and substitute teach. Their list hadn't been updated since 2004 since he hadn't subbed since then!

In an awkward and sad voice, Cecilia said, "Oh. Hi. This is Chris's wife. Um. He died last month."

As if she just said "he retired," the woman said, "Oh. Ok. We'll take him off our list." Then she hung up.

Camille then started asking questions.

"Mom, is Daddy coming home?" Her little, sweet, six-year-old voice sounded so full of hope. It broke my heart.

"No, baby, Daddy is in heaven, remember?"

Imagine your six-year-old overhearing a phone call for her dead father. The child was so confused.

Later that day, I got a call from Cecilia.

"So, I felt the need to call the school back."

"Oh my. Give me the play by play," I said.

"I said, 'Hi. This is Christopher's wife. You called me earlier to ask if he could sub?'"

"Yes, I remember. I took him off our list."

"Well, Chris was thirty-five-years-old, not some old man who passed away. He fought a hard battle with cancer, but in the end lost. Your phone call was upsetting to my daughter and me this morning. You should be more sensitive when you call people.

"Her response was priceless, but in an asshole sort of way.

"She said, 'Yes, that happens a lot when I call people. Lots of times the person is retired or dead. I'm used to it. Like I said, he's off the list so that you won't hear from our school again. You might want to call other schools to let them know, so you don't get any more calls that upset you.'

"Oh really! Should I? Is that what I should do?" I wasn't sure if Cecilia said that last part or if she was just saying it after the fact.

"You should have said, 'Fuck you! I bet your husband didn't die of cancer. What's that? You're not married?!? Shocking. You seem like a super sensitive person. I can't imagine why no one would marry you!'"

This got her laughing.

Cecilia started to joke with me, "Hey, Jen. You know that guy who took me to prom? Yeah, he died."

Laughing so hard, I spit out my freezing cold coffee that I never drank in the morning and was now on my desk at work. I decided to join the game.

"Hey, Cec. You know that guy who got mad at you for not having enough change to buy two donuts because you used all your money on a meter, so you had to split one donut instead of each having your own? Yeah, he died."

We went on like that for an hour. It felt good to joke, but also to remember some pretty funny and special times.

"You know that guy who would have told the insensitive woman from that school that she was dead to him? Yeah, he died."

Rich and I don't like to fight in front of the kids, so we lock ourselves in the closet and "whisper yell."

One time, when visiting my parents and they disagreed about something, our kids asked, "Aren't you going to go to the closet to do that?"

Chapter Fourteen

WE ALL LIVE BUSY lives. The girls are always busy, and I'm always busy. When did this happen? It used to be that we'd say, "Let's meet for dinner." And we'd meet the next night. Now we have to plan months in advance to get all four of us together and then inevitably someone can't make it for some reason or another.

I don't know when life got so busy, but I seem always to have shit to do. If it's not for work, then for the kids, or the house, or my family that lives far away, or a friend or, or, or. I have a headache just thinking of all the things I have to do. When I lay my head on my pillow at night, I grade myself for my day's work. Either I get an "A" because I am a hero for getting all this stuff done in one day. Or I give myself an "F" because I am a fucking failure and why can't I get my shit together? It varies day to day which is not good for the self-esteem. I'm a full-time teacher, Mom, and wife (the order of importance varies daily). People always say, "My kids come first." I call bullshit! I don't know anyone who can drop everything that is required of them to give 100% of their attention to their children or their spouse. It's not possible. We are only capable of so much and hearing people say that pisses me off because they say it to make themselves feel better and make you feel like shit. The fact is, too much is placed on us on any given day, and no matter how much we wish we could give 100% to our kids, I'm sure it is a dream …

My life consists of running from one thing to another. I run out the door at 6:45 every morning with two kids ready for school. I get to work at 7:30. I teach with as much energy as I can muster, then at 2:30, I am off to be "Mom," leaving a million things at work to wait until recess and lunch the following day. I run to take the kids to their activities, do homework, or run errands. I get dinner on the table no later than 6:00 (after we get home, which is 5:00 if we had errands or an activity). After dinner, I read to my kids (insert dream here, wishing it could be every night but secretly lying that I, a reading teacher, reads with my kids every night), make sure they take showers and by 8:00 they are asleep, and I pass out! On the day my kids are at dance or karate I have exactly fifty minutes to run and pick up a prescription, go to the post office, pick up dry cleaning, run to the grocery store to pick up anything I forgot on my weekly Sunday trip. That day is a whole other story … I could take those fifty minutes and sit and watch them dance and kick the ass of some kid in a karate match, but I feel like if I could get stuff done without having to drag them with, then I should take advantage of those precious minutes just to stay afloat.

This one particular day my daughter was at dance, my son in karate (thankfully they are right next door to each other) and I had to run to pick up my son's

ADHD medicine, pick up dry cleaning so my husband could have something to wear the next day, and mail out a package to my brother in Chicago. I realized I planned on making steak on the grill for dinner and had to get the steak. It would have been easier to get the steak on Sunday at the grocery store but my husband once bought meat at our regular grocery store, and it said on the label "Product of Chile, Mexico, Spain, and Portugal." They can't pinpoint exactly which country the meat came from? Is it a filet hybrid of sorts? Hence the reason we get our meat from Whole Foods. Luckily the UPS store, dry cleaner and Whole Foods were in the same shopping center as the kids' dance and karate place. So, strategically I ran to the pharmacy down the road, ran back and had forty minutes to do everything else. The cleaner, God love her, had it waiting for me. She always tells me I make her dizzy watching me run everywhere. Tell me about it. I'm dizzy just writing about it, and I live it every day! So I had exactly thirty minutes to go to Whole Foods.

When I walk through Whole Foods, I always notice everyone stopping to "smell the roses" shall we say. On this particular day, all the employees wanted to stop and chat and ask me about my day. I don't have time for this, I was thinking. Please just let me get my steaks and get the fuck out of here! I'm from Philadelphia and we Northeast people are rush, rush, rush, no-nonsense people. After the lady in front of me got a detailed ten-minute story on the lamb kabobs she was picking up I was ready to lose it. I kept checking my watch. Fifteen minutes to go. I was screwed. I was two doors away from my kids, and I was going to be late! I don't know about you, but I loathe being late. It produces so much anxiety in me. I always try to be early if not on time, especially for my kids pick up times. They don't have me all day. They deserve not to worry where I am and they deserve not to have to be dragged around the city so I can run these errands. They too have been gone since 6:45 in the morning and deserve to go home at a normal time to unwind.

"Hey. How can I help you on this fine day?"

I took a deep breath. It was finally my turn. "My day is fine. Thanks. Just really busy. Can I please have four filets?"

"Ah Filet. Someone is having a fancy dinner. What are you making with that?"

"Um, orzo and veggies," I replied in a clipped voice. I could sense my irritation growing.

"Awesome!" He started taking out the parchment paper to place on the scale to weigh the steaks.

"Do you know how much you want these babies to weigh?"

"Just anywhere between four to six ounces are fine." I started tapping my foot. I think it was my subconscious trying to get this guy to hurry up. I looked at my watch, trying to signal to him that I was in a rush.

As he was weighing the steaks, he was trying to make what I could only assume to be small talk.

"Did you know these cows were locally grown? They were grass fed their whole life! You ever see that documentary about the cows eating corn?"

Before he could finish, I said, "Listen, I know

you're just doing your job, and you're very nice. But I have to get to my kids in the next ten minutes."

"Oh, I get it. You need to get out of here."

Just then, another meat guy came over and whispered something in his ear. "I'll be right back," he said.

No! I have to leave. My heart was racing. I thought my eyeballs were going to pop out of my head.

"Just give me my fucking meat please!" I yelled. Not sure why I added the word 'please.' Maybe I was trying to make up for the fact that I just dropped the F-bomb in the middle of Whole Foods.

The guy looked dumbfounded and handed me the package of steaks.

"Hope your day gets better," he said. How embarrassing. I never lose my cool like that.

I walked over to the checkout line. The line felt like an eternity.

"Oh, I've been wanting to try this soap. It's the hemp and aloe one we just got," the cashier said.

"Yes! I love it. It smells amazing," the lady said.

"Oh and do you like this cheese? I haven't tried it yet," the cashier asked.

"I don't know. I've never tried it. It's my first time buying it," she said.

"I have, and it gives you the runs. Don't buy it," I blurted out.

The cashier and the lady just stared at me in disbelief. She told the cashier to put it back. The lady paid and awkwardly tried not to look at me.

Now it was my turn. The cashier just looked at me with such disappointment in her eyes.

I finally got out of there. As I walked to the karate and dance place to get the kids, I had exactly three minutes. I decided to call Cec. She picked up on the second ring.

"Is everyone in Whole Foods stoned but me?" I yelled.

"Jen, everyone in LA is stoned but you!" Cecilia responded.

Cec and I went to dinner, and I had just started a diet. I was ordering a salad and a plate of broccoli.

We started talking to an elderly woman next to us. She was commenting on what I ordered.

I said, "I'm going to look amazing in four months."

She replied, "Why? Are you having a face lift?"

Chapter Fifteen

"WE NEED A NIGHT out!" Cecilia declared to me on my way home from work. We got tickets to a nineties grunge band night at the Wiltern Theatre. A friend of ours ran the Wiltern and hooked us up with wristbands to get us in the pit during the show right in front of the stage. Another friend has a brother who is the lead singer of one of the bands playing that night, and she and a couple of other friends came too. We drove together. We were all meeting at my friend Cheri's house. I picked up Cecilia at her house so we could be together before heading over to carpool to the show.

I parked in Cecilia's garage. Ever since Chris passed away, Cec insisted I have the garage clicker and a key in case I needed to get into her house to rescue her from something. What that something was, I had no idea.

I let myself in and climbed the stairs of her multi-level townhome. I heard music coming from the third level and some loud, off-key singing. I made my way up to the top floor. I walked into Cecilia's bedroom to find her with her back to me in her bra and underwear singing at the top of her lungs

Madonna's "Love Don't Live Here Anymore" song from the '80s. I wish a book had audio so you could hear what I heard. It sounded like Madonna singing a duet with a bird whose neck was being squeezed.

> *You abandoned me*
> *Love don't live here anymore*
> *Just a vacancy*
> *Love don't live here anymore*

She was singing, dramatically to a picture of Chris. The whole scene was incredibly depressing and hysterically funny all at the same time.

"I thought we were seeing a '90s concert?" I interrupted.

She jumped and laughed at how I startled her. She handed me a hairbrush to use as a microphone, and we continued to wail the song at the top of our lungs together with an epic big finish. Now it was Madonna singing with two birds being strangled.

"They don't make music like they did in the '80s."

"No, Madonna doesn't make music anymore like she did in the '80s," I pointed out.

"True."

Cec continued getting dressed and finished her makeup as if I hadn't walked in on her in a vulnerable moment.

We drove over to Cheri's house and met up with a few other people. I drove because my car fits up to eight people. As we were getting closer, someone asked if I knew where to park.

"I know where to go. I saw the Nutcracker here! We're VIP!"

I don't know why, but I kept saying that. They made fun of me all night for bragging that I saw the Nutcracker there and had the Nutcracker hook up on parking. It was my friend Stacey who gave me the parking hook up.

Once we parked, we walked into the lobby of the theater. I took notice of what everyone was wearing, pleased with my outfit. I ran out and got a Nirvana shirt. I went to H&M because I texted my friend Julie who knows all things fashion and she told me H&M would have something. I searched all through the store and found it!

The shirt reminded me of this guy in high school I pretended to like Nirvana for all so he would hang out with me. I didn't even know who they were. I was a musical theater geek. I'm sure he didn't know who Lea Salonga and Colm Wilkinson were, but then again it was me trying to impress him. The night we heard about Kurt Cobain's death was a turning point in our relationship and my acting career. I had to pretend to know who Kurt was, pretend to be devastated, and then pretend to know all of Nirvana's songs. I must say, I pulled it off and the next few months had amazing amounts of make out sessions. But it was not meant to last.

I paired my new shirt with jean shorts and combat boots. I applied thick eyeliner and, for one night, got to feel like I was sixteen again.

We went into my friend Stacey's office where she

had a whole bar set up! We all had some drinks and hung out chatting away. We then headed out to the stage.

The first band wasn't that great, so we decided to visit my friend's brother backstage. We took pictures together and got to chitchat for a few minutes. Cecilia and I didn't want to go back to the show yet. We decided to go sneaking around the upstairs of the theater making each other giggle like schoolgirls. I'm not sure why we were giggling. Maybe it's because it was so out of character for us to break the rules.

As we wandered the abandoned hallways of the upper level of the theater, we were convinced we were going to get arrested or attacked by a ghost. It would have been a famous musician ghost, which would have been exciting but scary too. It was the thought that if we got caught, how good that sounded. An arrest would have been a nice break away from our kids. That's fucked up to say, but we were fantasizing about how we wouldn't have to make breakfast in the morning because we'd be in jail. Yes, we are twisted, but doesn't a break sound nice? I mean the accommodations aren't a suite in Barbados, but …

When we got back to the stage area, a new band was there and a mosh pit formed. Cec and I tried to "join" but we were just trying to survive in the crowd. What had we gotten ourselves into? Why did we decide to come back down from our haunted fantasy upstairs? Cecilia ended up getting banged and thrown into the stage by this unapologetic man who didn't care that I was then giving him dirty looks and saying he was an asshole. When the guy smashed into her, and she looked hurt, something possessed me. I wanted to punch the guy. I wanted to tell him what a fucking douche he was.

"Hey! Her husband just died!"

Why? Why did I yell that?

"Really? Out of all the things you could say, that's what comes out of your mouth?"

Laughing, "I guess I could have yelled, 'watch it Twinkle toes.' Would that have been better, Cec?"

"Mosh Pit Dancer."

"Dancer? Really?"

"OK, OK, OK. Let me think. Ummm … got it! 'Hey, this isn't Solid Gold'!"

After the Mosh pit incident, we decided to visit my friend's office again to refill. The drinking continued, and we proceeded to get more and more tipsy. We headed back to the stage to see my friend's brother perform. Another band we knew was on, and we were singing along and having a fantastic time. There was this guy standing next to us getting kind of flirty. Cecilia, being recently widowed, needed lots of practice talking to the male species again … so I grabbed the opportunity. After the band had finished we spoke to him for a while until the next band came on. We started dancing and singing while the band performed. The guy we were talking to asked us if we could pose for a picture. So we did.

"Oh my God. You girls are so much hotter in a picture than you are in real life!" he said.

"Wow. That is the rudest and funniest thing ever

said to us in our lives!" I exclaimed. "I mean, who says that?"

I feel like you can't get the full experience reading it, but I am telling you, he looked at us, snapped the camera, looked to review and said with a dead face, "You girls are so much hotter in a picture than you are in person." We laughed so hard until…

"Hey. Do you two want to go grab something to eat with me after the show?" Mr. Photographer asked.

"This would be a perfect opportunity to puke on your shoes," I said.

"I take that as a 'no'?" he mumbled.

"Uh? Ya think?"

My son spent an entire day convincing my daughter she had super powers. The next morning at breakfast she screamed, "AIDEN! You lied to me! I sent out two laser beams, and nothing happened!"

Aiden, who forgot his previous day's mischievous prank, casually said, "No Jossie. Remember, Mommy is here, and your powers don't work if Mom is around."

She bought it and retained her "Powers."

Chapter Sixteen

MY SON WAS DIAGNOSED with ADHD. This was not an easy thing to go through, acknowledging that our child might have this issue. I've seen parents struggle through it for years, as a teacher. When it was my turn to look at it through "parent eyes," I realized what my students' families had gone through. It's not easy to decide to give your eight-year-old medicine. It's not easy to teach an eight-year-old how to swallow a pill.

I'll never forget when we decided to try medication for our son. After the second day on this medicine, my husband turned to me and said, "We've lost him." The medication made Aiden such a zombie. He was not acting at all like himself. He just seemed drugged for lack of a better way of describing it. After a call to the doctor, she explained that it was the right diagnosis but wrong medication. So we switched to another type, figuring we could give it one more try and it has changed our whole family. This new medicine allowed Aiden to still be wonderful, goofy Aiden but with the ability to stop and think. Our relationship with our son has changed, our family life and his relationship with his sister has changed. It's been an amazing transformation for our family, and I felt bad that I hadn't done it sooner.

But now I have twenty-eight pills of ADHD medicine that he will never use. The medicine that didn't work for him was just sitting in my house. It was just sitting there with no one to help.

I had heard about people who take this stuff because it makes you super productive. It's also supposed to make you not hungry. You are basically on speed. That's what I heard, anyway. I know, I know. I'm such a hypocrite. I judge others for smoking weed, but I don't hesitate in trying my son's prescription pills. I have no defense other than I'm an ass.

If you don't have ADHD and take the medicine, it makes you hyper. Well, cut to me going out with Panooch and Cec not too long after the Grunge Band night. Cec and I went to this screening of a movie that a friend of mine from college was a part of. We had a couple of glasses of wine, mingled, and then left to meet up with Panooch and another friend at a local pub in Hollywood.

I hadn't eaten much that day, because, I can now attest to, the medicine does make you not hungry. To say that the pills and alcohol don't mix well would be an understatement.

Let's just say; I was caressing my own skin and saying how smooth it was! I started taking selfies like I was a model. I looked down and realized my glass was empty. I hopped down off the stool and went over to the bartender. I ordered, and it was like the bartender slid me my new drink within three seconds.

"You are the fastest bartender! I mean, you should, like, be a bartender, you're so good. You make the best cosmos ever. You should be a bartender!"

All the while I was caressing my face like I was a newborn baby. He looked at me like I was insane and I walked back to my table. I set my drink down and attempted to hoist myself up on the stool. My body felt like lead. I gave it all I had and somehow ended up on the floor, hysterically laughing at myself. Panooch helped me up, and the girls decided it was time to take me for a burger and fries. I couldn't walk by myself, and I was complaining, "I can't eat because I never eat after 8 p.m."

"I'm gonna be fat, now. Is that what you guys want? You want me to be fat?" This was slurred and I was attempting to cry. The girls just shrugged my protests off and guided me to the restaurant.

When we got there, they ordered me a burger and sweet potato fries. Honestly, food had never tasted so good. I devoured the entire thing, and in five minutes I was normal. It was as if the food was a secret potion waking me up from some spell that was put upon me. It was the weirdest night ever.

Lesson learned.

I will never take the medicine again! There's a reason it should only be given to those who need it. Back to my judgmental self.

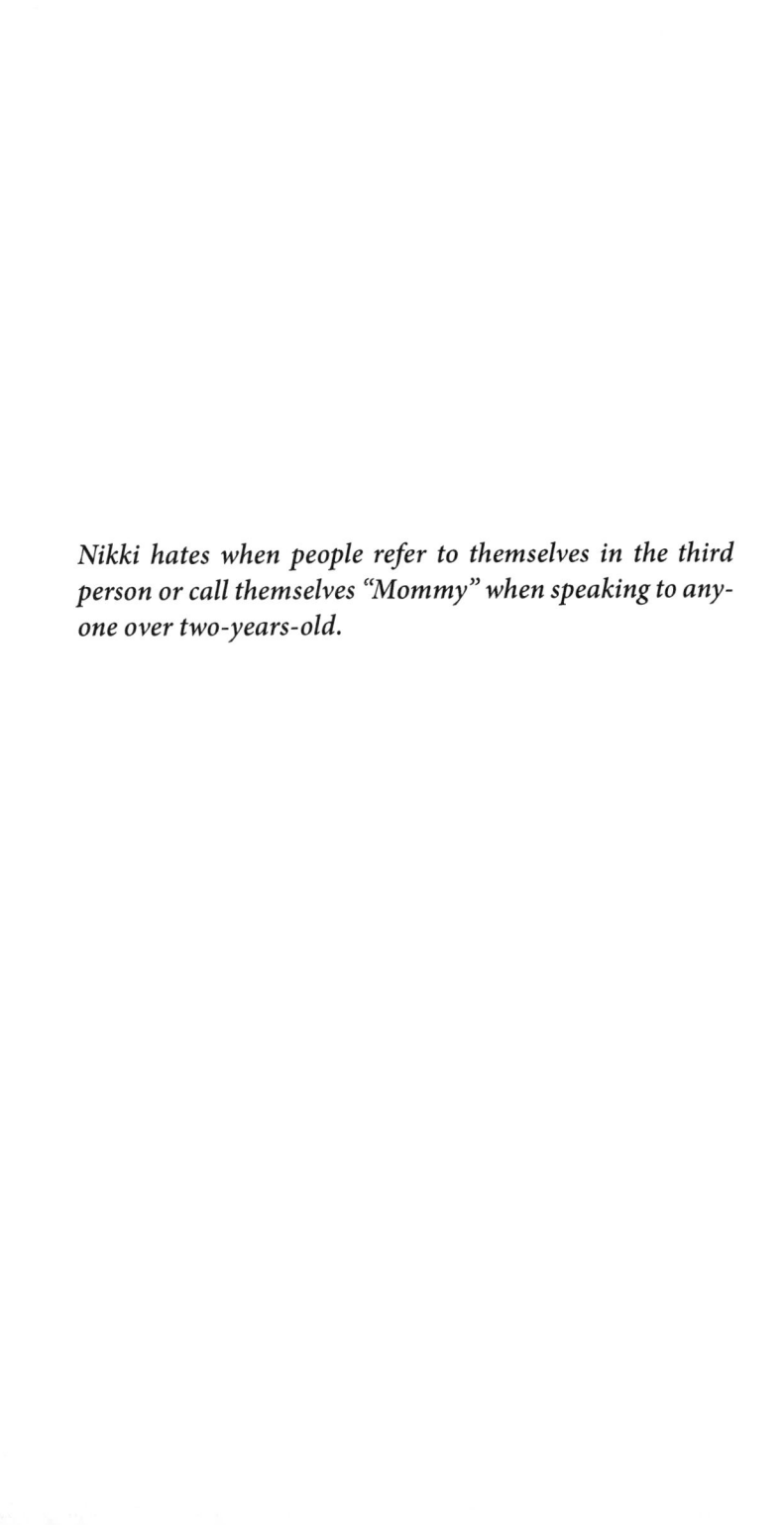

Nikki hates when people refer to themselves in the third person or call themselves "Mommy" when speaking to anyone over two-years-old.

Chapter Seventeen

Nikki and Tommy are in a band, hence, why they sang at Chris's memorial service. They are talented. I could listen to them all day. As a matter of fact, I do. I have a CD with songs they wrote, and I listen to it over and over again in the car.

Their shows are fun. They are always in cool, trendy places. Nikki is mesmerizing to watch on stage. You feel like you're just having a conversation with her as she sings to you and jokes around between songs. She's so real. She is not afraid to laugh at herself, doesn't take herself too serious, and makes everyone feel like she is connected to them.

I brought my parents to a show of theirs once. My parents think Nikki walks on water. She was drinking beer in between songs and let out the biggest belch I had ever heard! It got even louder because she realized it would be entertaining if she did it into the microphone.

"Nikki!!! My parents are here!" I shouted at her from the audience.

She just shrugged her shoulders, winked at my dad.

My dad attempted to explain to me why Nikki could burp like that.

"She can belch like that because she has a strong diaphragm from being a singer."

Really? If I did that in front of my dad, he would not be making excuses as to why it was acceptable. Like I said, she walks on water.

I decided it was time to go out again with Cec. She was talking to some guy from high school, but it wasn't anything more than talking to someone who knew her back when she and Chris were dating. But she needed to put herself out there. This was something she was not comfortable with. She just wasn't ready. I had to respect her feelings.

We decided to go see Nikki and Tommy's show. It was in a small theater in Santa Monica. It was a cool show because they had a comic, a beat boxer, and a harp player there that night.

We got there early and were waiting out in the front hall before the doors opened for the show.

We were standing around talking when all of a sudden this guy breezes past us. He abruptly stopped, walked backward, and paused in front of us. Without so much as a word, he went right up to Cecilia and smelled her neck! I mean literally went up to her and ran his nose up her neck! You think she's awkward talking to strangers? Imagine a random guy smelling her. That shit was funny. Her face was priceless. It was a combination of grossed out, bewildered, and deer in headlights.

He then announced, "Chanel. You're wearing

Chanel. I'd know that smell anywhere!" Cec just stood there laughing out of pure awkwardness.

"I know every perfume! I am a professional perfume identifier. My ex-girlfriend wore the same perfume. I'd know that smell anywhere."

I made some snarky remark.

"Ex-girlfriend? I'm shocked."

Cecilia was speechless.

After a few silent moments, she told him he was wrong, and it was some other perfume. He kept trying to talk to her until the doors opened. We found a couch where another girl was alone. We sat next to her figuring we would be safe from "smelling man." We started talking to this girl, and it turned out she was the wife of the harp player. We told her what happened to Cecilia and she made us show her who the guy was. We couldn't find him. Then the lights went down, and everyone clapped and in walked THE GUY onto the stage! He was their opening act! Oh, my God. He was a stand-up comic. I couldn't tell you if he was funny or not because we were laughing that he was the smelling guy. Our new friend, Em, was laughing along with us. The guy did his bit and then was introducing Nikki and Tommy.

Nikki and Tommy came on a little bit later and were amazing as always, and the show was great. I couldn't wait to tell Nik what this guy did.

After the show, we ended up going for coffee with Em. We hit it off and were all excited to have made a new friend. As we were talking, we looked over at the table next to us. I don't know why we all did it at the same time, but we did. Maybe we saw it from the corner of our eyes, or maybe it was intuition, but there was a woman sitting there. She had a big purse. Out of her purse came a watermelon. She then took out a knife and proceeded to cut the watermelon in half and ate it. She pulled out a large spoon and was eating a watermelon in the middle of a coffee house!

It reminded me of the scene in Dirty Dancing when Baby says, "I carried the watermelon." Except a woman was eating a melon, out of her purse, in the middle of a restaurant. Maybe "Smelling Guy" and "Watermelon Girl" can develop a new, delicious, fragrance together.

Divorce and death are not the same

Chapter Eighteen

TIME WENT BY. MONTH after month and, pretty soon, it's been a year and a half since we lost Chris. It felt like yesterday and an eternity all at the same time.

Cecilia had never been with anyone else besides Chris, and it certainly had been a while since Chris passed since she had any physical, male contact. It was time for her to get out there and try to meet someone to spend time with and start living again. It took a little convincing, but she agreed.

A friend of hers knew someone who had lost his wife and thought they might have some common ground. Cecilia agreed to talk to the guy on the phone. She called me after they spoke.

"They were in the middle of a divorce! It's not the same. He doesn't get to be as upset as I am!"

She decided to try the whole Match.com thing. I helped her fill out her profile. She went out with a couple of people but never more than once. Her dates went something like a round of speed dating parties. Picture a dark restaurant with booths. Cecilia was sitting on the comfortable black leather. Her outfit had been hand crafted by my husband and me, through a FaceTime consultation. She was wearing a black top with white, skinny jeans, sandals, and of course, a visit to the dry bar had happened earlier in the day.

Round 1:

"Hi. I'm Cecilia. It's so nice to meet you."

"Cecilia? That's a beautiful name. How is it that such a beautiful girl is still single?"

Cec, who is never prepared for what to say in such a situation, tries to make a joke.

"Oh. Well. That's a funny story. Not funny ha-ha, but funny, like, you know. Well, um. My husband died."

Round 2:

"So Cecilia. Where are you from?"

"Um, I grew up here in LA. I grew up in the valley."

"So glad you could come out. Your profile said you have a daughter. Is it her dad's weekend?"

"That's a whopper of a story. So my husband died, but I'm fine. Seriously I am fine."

Round 3:

"So let's just get this out and in the open. And I want you to know I'm OK with this." She takes a deep breath, "My husband died."

The guy's mouth is on the floor; his eyes are as wide open.

Cut straight to Cec, sitting on the same side of the booth with some stranger, while he is crying his eyes out on her shoulder.

"That's so horrible. He was so young and left you so early."

After a bunch of doozies and a guy who even stood her up, she found out our housekeeper was on Match.com and was getting more dates than her. She was so pissed! So she took a break from the whole online dating thing.

It was now February. Another anniversary was approaching of Chris's passing. Just when you least expected it, Cecilia ended up meeting someone she knew during a Super Bowl party. It was safe and familiar, and she didn't have to explain about how her husband had died.

With this friend, there was no need to explain. He knew her from years ago, knew Chris passed away, and it was for lack of a better word, safe. They started hanging out and began having major make out sessions. It was the first time she had been kissed in a long time. She was excited to explore this new side of herself. Who was she now, at thirty-six, without Chris? She wanted to be uninhibited and not judge what was happening. She was living in the moment. These, of course, were her words.

"I'm just having fun. There's no judging here. We'll see what happens," she said confidently.

One night she went to his place, and they started kissing. As the kissing heated up, they started to move down the hall. When they reached his bedroom, she saw he had a Captain America blanket on his bed!

She was telling me about it during one of our "Coffee Talks."

"I was like, 'Ok, yeah, sure we can do this on your Captain America blanket. That's not weird or creepy at all that a grown man still has that.' But ... why does he still have that?"

"I don't know. Rich collects Spider-Man comics. Maybe that's his thing?"

"I just couldn't have sex on his Captain America blanket, but Jen it's been over two years!"

"You know what you could do? Send Cam over to your mom's so you can have him over to your house."

Famous lines by Cecilia:

"I've been dieting all day. Am I skinny yet?"

"Tan=skinny!"

"I'm a Vegan. Just not today."

Chapter Nineteen

THE NIGHT OF OPERATION Get Cec Laid, Panooch and I had dinner plans. We met at this super yummy and trendy pub in Sherman Oaks. No matter where we are, without fail, she gets hit on. The entire meal the server was overly attentive to her, ignoring me. I'm used to it. Nicole is beautiful, tall, skinny, and has an angelic face. Her eyes are the shape of cat eyes, and she accentuates them with blue eyeliner. She is strikingly beautiful. She looks like Katie Holmes and Ashley Judd, but hotter. People are drawn to her. It's one of the reasons I love her. If only I could have gotten a refill on my diet coke from Mr. Douche himself that was gawking at my best friend.

Anyhow, during dinner, Panooch got up maybe three times to go pee. I thought something was off. We go out all the time, and this was the first time she has needed to go to the bathroom that many times in one sitting in a restaurant. The server kept coming by and asking me different questions about her while she was gone. Sure buddy, now you talk to me. I told him she was married and he tried to play it off like he just wanted to be her friend. Ok. Sure.

We left the restaurant and weren't ready to say

goodbye, so we decided to go for a walk and look for a coffee house.

When we got there, Panooch had to pee again. "What is going on with you?"

"OK, you have to promise not to laugh at me."

"Of course."

"So I've been having a problem not being able to hold my pee. It's been since I was a kid. If I don't go as soon as I feel the urge, I pee all over myself."

It was funny. I started to laugh. Panooch is never one to want to talk about any bathroom problems. It embarrasses her. She's a lady and ladies don't talk about the potty. It's not sexy.

"I told you not to make fun of me!"

"I'm not. I swear. It's just ironic that this would happen to you of all people who hates talking about your private bathroom moments."

"I'm going to go. I'll be right back."

We were in one of those coffee houses where you need a key to get into the bathroom. Nicole went to grab the key, but someone had it already. She ran down the dark hallway. Whoever was already in there was taking forever. This was getting to the point where she couldn't hold it, and the person in the bathroom was NOT coming out. She had to make a quick decision: pee on the floor of the hallway or run out the back door to the back alley. She chose to run outside. She took a quick survey of the area. She saw it was clear and squatted down to pee on the ground. As she was taking a deep breath with relief that she didn't soil her panties, she looked up and saw a guy waving at her from a parked car. There was nothing she could do. She was mid-flow. Of all the people for this to happen to…my poor Panooch. She stood up and made as graceful an exit as she could.

She came back to the table where I was sitting, red-faced.

"I have to tell you something. But first, we have to leave. Now!" Her voice wasn't angry but urgent.

We got up to leave. I was confused why we needed to leave, but she looked pretty serious. She whispered in my ear what had happened. I think I laughed embarrassingly loud as she pulled me to the door. Just then, before we could open the door ourselves, a guy was coming in and opened it for us.

I walked out, but when he saw Panooch, he said, "Oh. Hi!"

She said in an awkward voice, "Hi."

She grabbed my arm and took off down the street.

"That was the guy! The guy who watched me pee!"

Just as we got to my car, my cell phone rang.

"Um … he can't keep it up!"

Nicole and I, both listening to my phone, looked at each other and lost it. Cecilia was calling us from her bathroom, whispering how this guy was having 'performance' issues. She didn't know what to do.

"This never happened with Chris! Ever! Is this kind of thing what happens to men these days? Is it all the organic milk? Maybe the hormones *were* good for people? Maybe he needs hormone milk? Is that a thing?"

The whole conversation was ridiculous.

Panooch chimed in, "Look, Cecilia, you have amazingly huge boobs. Let the guy 'motorboat' on them. That should lift him up!"

"Ok. Hold on. I'll go try."

Panooch and I just stared at each other. Was she leaving us on hold while she got this guy to motorboat her double D tits?

The next thing we hear is her saying, "Do you need a minute alone?"

A few seconds later, she got back on the phone.

"He's masturbating! I've never seen a guy do that before! Is this normal?"

Panooch and I laughed.

"I am so uncomfortable. I just excused myself so he could be alone."

"You need to get out of there!" I said.

"I can't leave! It's my house!!!"

"Oh, right. I forgot."

"What if I call your cell and pretend to be your mom and say Cami isn't feeling well and need you to pick her up?" Nicole suggested.

'Ugh. I'll figure it out. I gotta go. Love you. Bye."

"Why is she mad at us?" Nicole asked.

Somehow the guy left, and I remember telling Cecilia the next morning during our "coffee talk" that it would make a great story for way later and we would all laugh about it.

A couple of weeks passed, and Cec decided to give e-harmony a try. One late afternoon, I got a call.

"Yeah, Captain America is dating someone, apparently at work, now."

"You sound upset."

"I'm not upset. I'm … I'm …

" … upset?"

"I know!" She shouted.

I laughed. Cecilia is a walking Monica from Friends. She channels her inner Courtney Cox whenever she responds to me with 'I know'.

"Cec, the poor girl is suffering silently. And you know Captain America was not *the* guy."

"I know. I know. Anyway, I met someone on e-harmony. We passed the Q & A and email portion and are onto phone conversations. We're having dinner tomorrow!"

"Really!?! Wow! Awesome. What's his deal? Name? Where does he live? Do you think he'll like me?"

"Ok, everybody calm down," she said while laughing at me. She continued, "His name is Howard. He's divorced and has a son a little older than Cam. He lives in Encino."

"Oooh, Encino."

"And he has to love you. It's part of the package. Yeah, so we're just going to meet and have dinner and see."

"Wow! You sound so healthy."

She responded in her jokingly credulous voice, "I am. I really, really am."

Nikki's New Year's Resolution:

"I'm going to be less mean in 2015."

The next year ...

"I'm going to be less mean in 2016."

Chapter Twenty

"What if we show up there and sit in a corner?"

On the night of Cecilia's big date with Howard, I had dinner plans with Nikki.

"Right, like Cec could act like she doesn't know us? Please. She'll be cracking up and texting us from across the room," I said.

We were sitting at a table next to a window that opened up. The view was of the Valley's lovely Ventura Boulevard. Cars were rushing by. Pedestrians were walking. Bike riders were zooming down the street racing with the cars. The night was beautiful. It was summer hours, so the sun was still out and it wasn't too hot. It was the perfect evening.

"So what's going on with you?" Nikki always asks me this. I feel like I never have a good answer. My life is so predictable.

"Um. Nothing. My life is boring."

"Yeah, but how *are* you? How are you and Rich? Are you guys having sex?" Another question she always asks me.

"Yes, Nik. We are having sex," I answered rolling my eyes. This is a standard conversation with Nikki. I think she gauges my response each time she asks to decide how I'm doing and how Rich and I are. It's her way of checking in on me. I don't know any other person in the world that checks in with her friend this way, but that's what makes her Nik.

As we were talking, we were looking out the window and saw a woman pull up to a meter to park her car. Just as she opened her door, a biker was riding at full speed, hit the driver's side door and flipped over it and landed on the concrete, hard.

I can't tell you how many times I have been guilty of not fully looking if a biker is coming. I've never hit anyone, but still. It could have happened to anyone.

All the patrons in the restaurant who witnessed it gasped.

"Do you need us to call 9-1-1?" A woman yelled.

The guy waved at her and said no, he was fine. He was stretching his legs and checking his body for any stiffness or bruises.

The driver, in her defense (Nikki would kill me for defending her), did ask him if he was OK and offered to get his bike fixed.

Nikki was in full "Nikki Mode." She started yelling out the restaurant window at the woman.

"What? Your life is so important that you don't have to check for others? You don't care about anyone but yourself! You selfish bitch!"

The woman, I think, was trying to ignore the ranting woman yelling at her (AKA Nikki). She wouldn't even look in our direction. Can you imagine sitting in a restaurant with your best friend as she announced to the world what an asshole someone was outside? It is much like having her yell in the middle of Bloomingdale's that Kate Spade is robbing everyone! I tried to quiet her down. Everyone was looking at us. It just fueled her fire.

"No. I will not calm down! Assholes. People are fucking assholes. What are you all looking at?" She turned to me and continued, "You know, that's why I don't like people. Dogs, I like. And you. I guess I like you, too." She smirked.

The waiter came over to take our order. Nikki switched to sweet, cute Nikki.

'Thank you, dear," she said in a genuine, loving voice as he walked away.

"Thank you, 'dear'? What are you? Seventy?" I asked.

"I always say 'dear' to people. I'm a nice person. What do you say?"

"I don't know. 'Thank you?' My dad says 'dear,'" I said in an annoyed voice.

"Well, your dad is a nice person." Apparently, *he* walks on water too.

"I've never heard you say that in all the years we've been friends," I told her.

"You know who doesn't call people 'dear'? That bike murderer outside!" She started to raise her voice.

"Nik, the guy is fine, and I think he got her number."

"Well, then he's stupid because she's a self-absorbed asshole who only thinks of herself."

My spunky little girl purrs like a kitten but bites like a lion.

We got a text from Cec that everything was going great and they were making plans to see each other again!

"Oh my God! A second date! It's happening!"

One morning, a month after my daughter's sixth birthday, my son woke her up and said, "Happy Birthday!"

He convinced her it was her birthday again and told her it was OK to eat icing for breakfast. He told her not to wake me because I was still asleep and assured her that I had told him to make her morning special.

When I came downstairs, I found her eating icing out of the container for a cake I was making for his baseball team.

"Mom! Why didn't you tell me it was my birthday?!?"

Chapter Twentyone

My daughter was in a dance class once a week. It was nice because it was right by our house. I work thirty minutes away from home, and my kids come with me to the school where I work, so it's great to meet new people who live near us. One family my husband and I had gotten to know and even had over to our house for dinners. The odd thing was, whenever we had made plans, the wife never came. She was either working or didn't feel well. I didn't think anything of it. She is a doctor, and I always assumed, busy. The dad, Ben, works from home and is the one always running the kids to their after school classes.

A couple of times after class, Ben and I would run and grab dinner with the kids together. We both needed to feed the kids, it was late, Rich was working, and his wife was working so we just would go together. One time we both ran over to the grocery store at the same time and wound up grocery shopping together with the kids. It was funny when we'd bump into people we knew, and they'd make a comment that he got a new wife or I got a new husband. It was all meant as a joke and Rich laughed about it. We all joked one time at my house when having dinner and the kids were playing that we were a blended family. Ben and Rich got along well and made plans a few times for "guys night" to go check out a new band or grab a drink. Ben would call us and invite us to go to Disneyland when they were going because we all had annual passes. We never were able to all go because of our crazy schedules. Until ….

Spring Break was approaching, and at dance class one day, Ben and I were talking.

"So what are you doing during Spring break?"

"Rich has rehearsals, but I have plans for each day."

"Of course you do," he said with a laugh. "You're so organized."

"I have to be. We're going to Disneyland; the kids have a play date at a friends' house while I get my nails done. I have a movie day planned with an old student of mine while the kids play with friends. We have park plans. We'll be busy."

"Hey, would you mind if we came to Disneyland too?"

"Sure! That'll be fun. My kids will be so happy to be with your kids. You know Rich won't be there, though, right?"

"That's fine with me if it's fine with you … and Rich."

"Oh, he won't mind. We can drive together. I have a DVD player in my car so the kids can watch a movie while we drive down there."

"Cool. What time would you like to leave?"

"We go early. Seven?"

"Wow! Seven? That's great. When we go, we never

leave until eleven because I can't get my wife out of the house before then."

I laughed. "Oh. No. We have a whole plan for Disney. We leave early, get on all the rides we want. Rich and I even divide and conquer where he'll take the kids on one ride while I wait in another line that's super long. Or he runs to get fast passes while I take the kids on a ride. We have a system."

"Sounds great. Can't wait."

Monday morning came. Ben sent me a text that he was at Starbucks and asked for my order. 'What a nice guy,' I remember thinking. He pulled up at 7:15.

"Sorry, I'm late."

"You're forgiven. You brought me coffee." I smiled and took a tentative sip.

"Where's Carly?" I asked. Carly is Ben's three-year-old.

"Oh, I had the nanny take her to preschool. She wouldn't make it all day and night. It's just Kiley and me. It's better this way."

Hmmm. Ok, I guess Ben and I were taking only three kids to Disneyland.

We got on the road, and the kids decided to watch Frozen.

As we were driving, we talked.

"Do you know how amazing it is that I was able to get out of the house so early and head to Disney on the schedule we set?" he said.

"Really? Is that a hard thing for you?" I asked.

"Are you kidding? Karen likes to sleep in on her day off. She's leisurely. Watching you pack up the car made me think of yesterday when she texted me from upstairs to bring her the laundry basket because she was too sore from Pilates. You guys are very different. I watched you load the car and was shocked you didn't have Rich do it or ask me to do it."

I felt bad for the guy. He kept going on about how many things his wife complained about and never wanted to go anywhere or do anything.

"I hope you don't find this too forward, but have you ever gone to therapy? When Rich and I weren't on the same page about stuff, it helped to talk to someone. Marriage has its ups and downs. Believe me; there have been plenty of times when I wanted to kill Rich or leave. Or kill him and then leave him." I laughed at my joke, trying to lighten the mood.

"Oh, I don't think we'd be married anymore if we didn't have kids. We went to therapy one time, and Karen just complained the whole time that I sold my company and lost a lot of money."

"What did the therapist say?"

"She wanted to know how I made that kind of money in the first place and how I lost it."

"Sounds like the wrong therapist."

Eventually, we talked about more trivial things, like sports and the kids' schooling. I tried to keep it a light and easy conversation. I wasn't uncomfortable, but it was a little awkward knowing how unhappy this guy was in his marriage and I was his "companion" for the day.

We pulled into the parking garage, and we got over to the Magic Kingdom. Our first ride was Star Tours.

After the ride, we exited through the store and passed a t-shirt I have always loved.

"That's the shirt I love! I always pass it and tell Rich I want it. It says seventy-seven on the back, which is the year I was born. I love it!"

"So why don't you get it?"

"I don't know. Rich always talks me out of it."

The truth was, I did love the shirt, but for $40 I could buy something else that I'd love and wear more often. If I wanted it, I'd buy it.

We continued on more rides and then around noon decided to head over to California Adventure for lunch. They have the Boudin Bread Company there, and I love their chili in a bread bowl. I look forward to it every time we come to Disneyland.

Well, we get to the place, and they no longer have the chili!

"What!?! Ugh, that's annoying," I said in a little bit of a valley girl voice.

"Hey, I know a place where they have chili. Watch the kids. I'll be right back."

Before I could stop him and tell him it wasn't a big deal, he was gone. Really, I was a bit dramatic. I mean, I could have just had a taco at the Mexican restaurant and been fine.

I decided to text him.

Me: You didn't have to go running off on a chili manhunt. I'll be fine.

Ben: It's not a big deal. I'll be back in a sex.

Did he just text the word "sex"?

Ben: I mean sec! OMG I am so sorry.

Now I regret this next response. It sent the wrong message. I was only joking ... in a flirtatious, stupid way that now that I look back on it, it was idiotic of me.

Jen: Are you sure you made a mistake?

I remember thinking, "This is dangerous. Don't send things like that." Before I could type "just kidding" his response came through.

Ben: Oh! Can I buy you dinner first? LOL.

Jen: Looks like you're buying my lunch.

I feel like I am in confession. I honestly was joking around, but I was leading this guy on.

Fifteen minutes later, Ben came back with a chili cone from Carsland. He then went into the bread factory place and bought a bread bowl and voila! I had my bread bowl chili.

"I can't believe you just did that! Thank you. Rich would have told me to get over myself." Why was I throwing my husband under the bus? I know good and well, that if I wanted something, Rich would get it for me, like the Star Wars shirt. He knew I didn't *really* want it. But I had to admit; it felt nice to be taken care of. I am always so busy taking care of everyone else. This day felt easy in a weird way. A guy was paying attention to my needs.

After lunch, there was the parade. Ben went to get us some drinks. There's alcohol for sale at California Adventure. When he got back, he sat behind me on the crowded curbside.

"Does your backpack hurt?" He started to reach for my shoulders. Alarm bells started ringing in my head. I pulled away and made it look like I was just readjusting how I was sitting on the curb.

"I'm great! Thanks," I said in a light, clipped tone. Then came Aiden, my super intuitive son who misses nothing.

"Are you guys on a date?" Aiden asked.

Nervous laughter and with an incredulous voice, "What? Aiden, Ben is our friend. I love Daddy. I don't date other people. I'm married." I said the last part and looked at Ben. He laughed the whole thing off too.

"Yeah, little man. We're just all here having a good time. You're having a good time, aren't you?"

And then in typical Aiden fashion, again, he says, "Holding my mom's chair out, making sure she had chili, offering to carry her backpack ... aren't those things you would do on a date?"

"I'm just here to be your friend and your mom's friend."

Even though in the back of my head I knew this was also a little odd, it was a nice feeling because I am always on my own with the kids. I am jealous of women who have their husbands around, who are on regular schedules, or who have family close by to help them. It's hard being married to someone in the television industry and having most of your family across the country.

But as the day went on, the good feeling changed to uncomfortable because it didn't feel like two friends at Disney together with their kids anymore. It did feel like a date.

We went on a bunch more rides and decided to head to the Magic Kingdom to go on Splash Mountain one more time. I had promised the kids.

After the ride, I took the girls to get changed into their pajamas. Aiden changed in the men's room. Ben had asked if I minded if he ran to a store to get his little one a gift at a gift shop.

"No I don't mind at all, but you know we'll pass a bunch on Main Street on our way out."

"I don't want Kiley to see that I'm getting something for her sister. I'll be real quick."

"Ok. We'll meet you at the Walt Disney Statue."

"I'll be quick," he said again.

Twenty minutes later, Ben appeared at the statue and we all walked to the tram. The kids were exhausted, asking us to carry them. When we got them to the car, they passed out before I could even put the car in reverse.

"Wow, they were tired!" I said, taking a deep breath. The day was almost over. I just had to drive one-hour home and this weird day could be over.

Ben reached into his bag and pulled out a plastic bag.

"This is for you."

For me? I was confused for a second, and then I noticed the yellow lettering on the contents of the bag.

"What!?! Ben, you didn't? Is this the …

And there it was; The Star Wars T-shirt. Size Medium, 77 on the back, and my jaw on the ground. I was speechless until I wasn't.

"I can't accept this."

"Oh come on. You wanted it. I just want to see you happy. I'm in a position to give you something you want. I'd do that for any of my friends."

In hindsight, I should have insisted that I couldn't take it, but I was surprised and exhausted and emotionally confused. The day was so strange and getting stranger by the minute.

"Well, then thank you, my friend, for the thoughtful gift. I will wear it tomorrow and remember a fun day at Disney. Karen is lucky to have such a thoughtful, attentive husband." I threw in the line about his wife so he would know how aware I was that he was, in fact, married.

As we drove in silence, my mind drifted. I was thinking about how I was going to explain all of this to Rich. I didn't do anything wrong, per se, but I didn't think this was the kind of friendship we wanted from this family.

Out of the blue, Ben asked me, "Have you ever considered being with anyone else?"

Ok, he was not reflecting on the same thing I was. I was shocked.

"Do you mean while I'm still married?" I asked him, hopefully sounding disgusted by the question.

I needed to clarify before I assumed a guy who I thought was my husband's friend was hitting on me.

"Yes," he said simply. I could feel him staring at me.

I knew I had to be direct with my response. I looked him in the eye, only taking my eyes off the road for a second.

"I would NEVER cheat on my husband."

I looked back at the road.

I then continued to say, "If I felt there was something missing in my marriage, I would go to counseling or leave."

We sat in silence.

The rest of the ride was silent. Thankfully it was only another ten minutes to my house, where his car was.

We got out of the car and busied ourselves with unpacking the bags and kids. I carried my daughter upstairs while he put his daughter in his car. I took my son in and put him in bed and ran back to the garage to get all the bags and close up the car. Ben grabbed my elbow, turned me around, put his hand on the back of my neck and started pulling me in. At that moment I was like, "What the fuck is happening?" I turned my face and let him kiss my cheek. I pulled away and said goodbye like a scared little puppy, running into my house.

He whispered, "I'll call you tomorrow."

Ugh. Was this happening?!?

I ran upstairs, straight into my bathroom, splashed cold water on my face and said in a whisper, "FUUUUUUCK!" Rich was sound asleep in our bed.

When I got up the next day, Rich had already left for work. I went about my day as if nothing happened, which was true. NOTHING happened! So why was I feeling guilty? The kids had play dates, and I had an appointment for a manicure. While sitting and getting my nails done, I got a text from Ben.

Ben: Hey. I know you must be tired. Want me to bring you a coffee at your nail place? I know how you take your coffee."

Stalker much? So I replied.

Jen: No. I'm fine, thanks.

I wanted to keep my response short, not wanting to continue this weird exchange anymore.

I called Cecilia and asked her if we could meet after she finished work. We decided to meet at a park with the kids so they all could run around playing while I laid my head in my best friend's lap telling her the story of 'Disneyland Gone Wrong.'

"Jen, you feel conflicted because you wished Rich was there treating you that way. It feels good to get attention from people. You and Rich have been together a long time. It's normal to get out of sync with each others' needs, especially when you throw work and kids into it."

"I know. I know," I whined.

"You need to tell him what happened and not only that, but why you feel so bad about it."

Ugh, why does she always know the right thing to say? I guess we're the voice of reason for each other. Panooch and Nikki are the voices of reason too. I just knew that Cecilia would give me a forceful but loving response. I laugh at the response I think I would have gotten if I had called Nik or Nooch.

That night, when we got in bed, I got the courage to talk to Rich. "Babe, if you ever went to Disneyland with Lani, would you buy her a t-shirt?"

OK, I admit it was out of the blue to bring up my friend, Lani and it did not make any sense. But I didn't know how to start this conversation. I couldn't use Nikki, Nicole, or Cecilia as an example because they were family to us, so he *would* buy them a t-shirt. So I picked a friend that we were both friends with who also had a Disney pass. Made sense at the moment. Maybe Rich and Lani would go to Disney together if I were unavailable. I don't know! I was grasping at straws here, people! My thinking was convoluted.

He looked at me like I was nuts and I proceeded to spill the story in bits and pieces, "Look, I met up with Cec today and she thinks I need to tell you because I wish it was you at Disney with me. I mean, you'd go look for chili for me if I wanted it, right?"

"Babe, you are not making any sense. What happened yesterday?"

"Ben tried to kiss me!" I blurted it out. Rich laughed, I think nervously. He kept looking at me as I spilled my guts about all of it.

"He offered to carry my bag, pulled my chair out, ran to get me a chili when the bread place didn't have it."

"Wait. What? They don't have chili at the bread place? We're not going there anymore."

That's Rich. He's more upset about hearing about the chili than a friend hitting on his wife. This is the same person who paused the TV when we heard about the hiker who cut off his own arm and propelled himself down a mountain. When the hiker found other people on the trail, they gave him all the food they had left in their bags. This was when Rich paused the show.

"This is crazy," Rich said.

"What's crazy? That he cut off his own arm and lived to tell the tale or that he propelled down a mountain with a homemade tourniquet?" I asked.

"No! These people offered him what they had left, and it was two Oreos? If you have two Oreos, you should have none. Who doesn't eat the last two Oreos?"

My husband is one of a kind.

I continued, "Forget about the chili! Ben, at the end of the night, went to get that Star Wars t-shirt I always say I want, while I was watching all the kids. He surprised me with it in the car. He asked me if I would ever be with someone else and I, of course, told him never! I love you! You're the only one I want buying me Star Wars shirts!" I was sobbing at this point. Rich put his hand on my shoulder, letting me know it was all going to be OK.

He said in a serious voice, "Babe, I don't think we can be friends with Ben anymore."

I laughed. You know the ugly kind of laugh with snot coming out and maybe even a little spit but from the mouth that has glycerin in it from the crying.

Rich is the only person on Earth that can get me laughing and forgetting about things when I am upset.

"Get Cec on the phone right now!" He said in a commanding but joking voice.

When she answered I put her on speaker.

"Your best friend is insane!"

Rich proceeded to tell Cec the story from the information I gave him.

"That was not the way we practiced you starting the convo off. How did Lani get wrapped up into this?"

We all laughed and talked for a while.

"Hey what's that noise I hear in the background? Are you watching tv?"

"Oh. No. It's Howard. He came over to hang out after I put Cam to bed."

"Oooh. Howard. He's over. At night. With you. Does he like Captain America? That's a deal breaker."

Giggling, Cec said, "No he doesn't. Good night. Call me tomorrow."

"Love you."

"Love you too."

"Me too!" Rich shouted.

That's when I knew Cecilia was going to be OK. Here I was, happy for my friend but needing to get back to feeling like a shitty wife and mom.

As I lay down to go to bed, I still felt awful. My marriage was fine. Rich and I can get through anything. But I knew my daughter was going to be losing a friend and not to mention how awkward dance class was now going to be. How was I going to tell this guy, who I liked being around (until he tried to kiss me, give me a Star Wars t-shirt, and offered to bring me coffee at my nail salon), that we couldn't be friends? I hate confrontation.

The next day I was taking my girlfriend's daughter to the movies. She and I read the same book and were excited when the movie came out. Yes, I am fifteen at heart.

While in the bathroom I got a group text to Rich and me from Cec.

> *Cec: Hey Rich ... I'm really craving a cappuccino ... I'm at work would you mind bringing one to me?!? Thanks ...*
>
> *Rich: Sure. I'll bring the t-shirt I just bought for you.*

Sure let them have their fun at my expense! I still had to face him next week at dance class.

Or now! As I was coming out of the bathroom at the theater, laughing at the text Rich and Cec just exchanged, of all the people to run into at the movie theater…

Ben walks in with his kids and another mom from their school and her kids to see some children's movie. The following are the text messages that were then exchanged between Rich, Cecilia, and me explaining how this encounter went down:

> *Me: Of all the people to bump into at the movie theater! Kay and I were coming out of the bathroom and Ben, and the girls were there, meeting another mom and her kids to see Rio 2! It was sooooo awkward. He went to hug me but I put up my hand and we high fived!*
>
> *Cec: Well clearly this guy has a binder full of married women.*
>
> *Me: It was so uncomfortable. The girls both ran to hug me. Glad Kay was there with me. It stopped him, I think. Or maybe I'm crazy. Both are possible Ok. Movie is starting. Talk to you soon. Have a good show Babe!*

Rich was working on a live reality competition show at the time and was live that night in just a couple of hours. I wasn't expecting a response from him, but … this is what I came out of the movie to …

Rich: I hope you weren't wearing the shirt he gave you!

Cec: HAHAHAHA

Rich: I'm liking Ben less and less each day

Rich: Ben's favorite movie is "Fatal Attraction"

Cec: "Indecent Proposal"

Rich: "Unfaithful"

Rich: "I Think I Love My Wife"

Cec: "What Lies Beneath"

Rich: Wow-that's a good one

Cec: I could go all night!

Rich: "Cheaters"

Rich: Jen's going to come out of this movie with a million texts.

Cec: I know!!! Hahahahaha

Cec: "The Last Seduction"

Cec: "The Scarlet Letter"

Rich: "Election"

Rich: "An Affair to Remember"

Cec: "To Die For"

Me: You guys are out of control.

Me: Ummm. He texted me during the movie, "I think I owe you an apology" Haven't responded! WTF! What do I do?

Rich: Maybe you'll get another shirt.

Cec: I have to watch "Fatal Attraction" again for a valid response. Please hold.

Me: Stop! What do I say?

Rich: He also owes me an apology.

Cec: and me

Me: Hahaha

Rich: Also he should apologize for texting during a movie

Cec: Hahaha

Rich: Also, I guess I owe Lani an apology

Cec: Ok real answer: Yes say the conversation was unacceptable and uncomfortable and leave it at that.

Me: You guys are literally killing me. I'm crying from you 2.

Rich: Maybe you shouldn't wear such revealing outfits to Jossie's dance class.

Cec: Like real tears or because Rich and I are hysterical?

Me: You guys are hysterical.

Rich: I'm more worried that she said we are literally killing her.

Rich: I just saw Cec's Fatal Attraction comment … awesome.

Rich: I start karate classes tomorrow.

Cec: Camille starts gymnastics tomorrow …

Jen: Ok I sent a response of "Thank you. I was feeling uncomfortable."

Rich: You thanked him?

Cec: For the shirt

Rich: That would make sense

Me: Here's his response, "For sure! I apologize if any boundaries were crossed. I didn't think about it until yesterday. It's totally my fault, and I truly apologize, and that will not happen again.

Me: Do I respond to that?

Rich: "The World According to Garp"

This exchange between the three of us still makes me laugh every time I reread it. I never did respond to

Ben's text and tried to put it all behind me. Maybe now things wouldn't be awkward. Wrong again!

∽∽∽

The following week I received the following text from Ben.

> *Ben: Hi Jennifer! I hope all is well and that your first few days back in school have been good. I really just wanted to say that I felt horrible about the text from last week. The last thing I would ever want is for anyone to feel uncomfortable especially you when it comes to me. I do realize that I was probably overly attentive at Disney but there was no ill intent behind it in any way! In all honesty I haven't been able to really be myself in years prob about 5 years to be exact. I know that sounds crazy but I really like to make people happy by doing things for them big or small and I can be very attentive at times because that's just how I am in general. It made me happy to be able to be like that and I felt like you genuinely appreciated which made me feel good about doing things. I didn't take the time to think about how those gestures could have been taken by you and for that I truly apologize. I just got caught up in the moment and I can't lie I really miss being that way for someone, and it be appreciated, but I honestly did not intend for you to feel uncomfy in any way. I'm hoping that you can*

truly accept my apology! You are one of the best people I know and really value our friendship. On another note, I'm assuming that the above info is what made you feel uncomfy but if I did something else besides that I would feel like a big fool (just kidding) but please let me know so I can apologize for that as well. Have a great rest of the day!

Now I had had enough. I decide to put an end to this. Here is my response:

Me: Ben, I appreciate your text and clarification. The bottom line is now it is uncomfortable, and I need to distance myself and my family. I wish nothing but happiness for you and your family and am sure we can be cordial when we see each other. But a line was crossed that makes me feel uncomfortable, and I don't see how things can go back to how they were. I love and respect my husband, and any friendship between us now would just seem disrespectful to him and our relationship. I hope you can understand that.

He responded right away.

Ben: For sure! I wish you and your family the best too.

I forwarded the response to Rich, wanting him to know that I put an end to this. We didn't need this drama in our lives! It was the group text strand with Cec again. Rich never responded to what I sent to Ben.

I decided to change the subject. A little while later, I asked Rich who got kicked off the results show he works on. His response is priceless:

Rich: Ben! Boom!

Cec: Drops mic (Chris Rock Style)

∾∾∾

Epilogue:

I HAVE THIS REOCCURRING DREAM ...
The scene is in a hotel room suite in Barbados. I've never been to Barbados, so my dream could be just a hotel in Puerto Rico or St. Thomas or Palm Springs. The air is salty and humid. Ok, it's not Palm Springs. Light is streaming through the curtains. A light breeze comes through the slightly opened sliding glass door with a balcony beyond that. Clothing is thrown all over the floor, but there is also a suitcase that has perfectly folded clothing in it. The sink in the bathroom is dripping slightly. In the distance, there are bells ringing. As the dream version of me drifts back to consciousness and I open my eyes, I realize I am in bed, naked, with my three best friends. How the hell did we get here? Why are we naked? And why is there a dog at the end of the bed sound asleep? Well, since Nikki and Nicole are there, the dog makes sense. They "rescued" it and when I say rescued I mean stole it from people who they deemed not worthy to take care of said dog. The clothing on the floor also makes sense because Cecilia hates to do laundry. The folded suitcase, clearly being mine, is my brain's way to keep order in the dream.

It's the same dream over and over. I never find out the answers to any of my questions. However, if I psychoanalyze the dream, I am a lesbian with dreams of running away with my three hot best friends. Or I am a middle-aged teacher, mother of two, wife of one, over worked, underpaid, wishing I had the chance to just stop and take a break.

Maybe my dream is no ordinary love story. But I have three amazing women in my life that I can talk to who won't judge me. And maybe that is all I need. Maybe I don't need all of America to agree with me or empathize with me. Maybe what I need, I already have.

I couldn't get through life without Nikki, Nicole, and Cecilia. They're my anchors. They're the ones I go to when something exciting happens or I'm having a terrible day. They're the ones that tell me I'm wearing the wrong lipstick shade or the wrong size pants. They're the ones I can tell that disgusting story to about the time I couldn't find a bathroom, had a stomach ache, was driving home with my kids, and had to pull over into a McDonald's to use the restroom because I shit in my pants like a one-year-old while my children announced to all of McDonald's that "Mommy pooped in her pants." Well, I guess I just told all of you reading this too, but I digress.

People evolve, friendships grow, and change and life keeps going.

But I have three amazing best friends. These are our stories. And life would suck without them.

A Note to The Reader

Dear reader,

A portion of the proceeds from this book will be donated to the Leukemia and Lymphoma Society in Chris's name. Thank you for your support in helping find the cure for these horrible diseases. One day we will find the cure and win the war on Cancer. In the meantime, Cecilia and I will rewrite the pamphlet on *How to be a Friend to a Cancer Patient* for my next book.

With Love and Appreciation,

Jennifer Preuss

Acknowledgments

Wow! I can't believe this book is finished! I have so many people to thank!

First, I'd like to thank my wonderful husband, Richard. Your support, love, and humor get me through life, daily! I love you.

To my two amazing kids: Thank you for being so patient with me (I almost wrote "Mommy" instead of "me" but don't want Nik to roll her eyes at me). Jocelyn and Aiden, you both are my reason for living. All the times I was away from you, writing, I'd like to think was making me a better mom for you both. I love you so much and hope my example will inspire you to always follow your dreams, no matter how long it takes you.

To the three inspirations of this book: Cecilia, Nicole, and Nikki. What can I say, that I haven't already said? This book is my love letter to the three of you. Your friendship and sisterhood over the years have shaped me into the woman I am today. I love you.

To Kelly, my amazing friend who told me I could write a book. I didn't believe you. You were so encouraging, inspirational, and patient with me. You taught me to find a process that works for me and see it through, no matter how long it takes. I will cherish your friendship forever. I struck gold the year I got to have your amazing daughter in my first-grade class and then Vanessa and you as my friends. I love you.

To Jenn Sterling, who told me to write as if no one was going to read it! That was the best advice I have ever been given. You have been such an inspiration to me ever since I read *The Perfect Game*. Your personal story of following your dreams helped me realize that it's never too late to pursue my passion. Thank you for inspiring me, writing for me (and all of the world), and for not thinking I was a stalker when I reached out to you on Facebook all those years ago!

To Alexis, for reminding me that I am a creative being. Your belief in me led to making one of my deepest dreams come true. When I started telling you about this story, you never once brushed me off or told me I was silly. You always encouraged me and took me seriously. I am honored to call you my friend.

To Caryn for getting me a meeting with a production company to share my stories with. That meeting was the first step to writing this book, and I am forever grateful. Your friendship and encouragement have meant so much to me.

Thank you N.W. for wanting to be my grammar checker and being enthusiastic about reading this book. You're an amazing friend. I love you, Kitten.

To Paige for reading this and giving me invaluable feedback and a great ego boost. You are an amazing person and friend.

To Lindsay for being such a supportive and encouraging friend. Thanks for jumping on board and giving me great advice.

Thank you to the real Jen P. I thought I was the real Jen P until I met you!

Thank you to my dad for giving me my sense of humor. I am so lucky to have someone to laugh with who "gets" my jokes. I feel like I have accomplished something when you laugh at something I say.

Thank you to my mom for being the most wonderful role model of all. When I was born, you were a nurse, and by the time I was nine, you were an attorney! I still don't know how you managed law school with kids, helping with homework, and having dinner on the table every night. Mark, Jeff and I think of you as Super Mom. You are my hero! I love you.

Thank you to my brothers and their wives and kids: Jeff, Sil, Carlo, Mikey, Emma, Mark, Amy, and Ella. I love you all and hope I make you as proud as you make me.

Thank you to my Mother-in-Law, Diane, for your endless support. I love you.

Thank you to my in-laws and all my wonderful family that I gained from marrying Richard. I love being a part of this family!

To Shannon and Glenn for helping me on the cover. Your advice is always spot on. Thank you for your friendship. I love you both.

To Matt … you know why.

To Growing Educators who I not only owe a thank you to for making me a more effective teacher, but for creating a writer out of me! Your weeks of study led me to try new things with my young writers. I then would go home and write and try out all the "craft moves" I was teaching my students during the day.

Finally, to all of you who purchased this book, thank you from the bottom of my heart. It took me a long time to get this book to a place where I was ready to share it with everyone. I hope you enjoyed reading our crazy 'life' stories. I never thought I was a writer. I still don't. I feel like I had important stories to share about love, loss, and friendship. I believe our stories are no greater than any of yours. I just got the nerve to write them down and share them. So go on and write your stories down! I'd love to read them.

∽∽∽

Please consider leaving a review for this book. However, as a teacher and a mom, I feel compelled to remind you that if you don't have anything nice to say, then don't say it at all. ;-) *#kiddingnotkidding*

Made in the USA
San Bernardino, CA
16 May 2017